T0198607

The
FIRST 50 PAGES

The FIRST 50 PAGES

ENGAGE AGENTS, EDITORS AND READERS,
AND SET UP YOUR NOVEL FOR SUCCESS

WD

WRITER'S DIGEST
BOOKS

JEFF GERKE

Writer's Digest Books
An imprint of Penguin Random House LLC
penguinrandomhouse.com

Copyright © 2011 by Jeff Gerke

ISBN: 978-1-59963-283-4

Edited by: Scott Francis
Designed by: Claudean Wheeler

DEDICATION

To Rod Morris
Mentor, friend, and first editor.
It's not a stretch to say that I owe my career to you
and whatever you saw in me way back when.

AUTHOR BIO

JEFF GERKE is a novelist and professional book doctor. He is popular at writers conferences across America as a fiction teacher. His style is informal and droll and tends toward the speculative. Jeff spent twelve years on staff at various publishing houses before launching his own small publishing company, Marcher Lord Press, in 2008. He writes under the pen name Jefferson Scott having authored such books as *Virtually Eliminated*, *Fatal Defect* and the Operation Firebrand series. His also the author of *The Art & Craft of Writing Christian Fiction* and *Plot Versus Character*. Jeff and his wife of more than twenty years have three children.

ACKNOWLEDGEMENTS

Thank you to Writer's Digest for the opportunity to help novelists better do what it is they're aspiring to do. It's such an honor to contribute to the library of books that have helped generations of novelists—and to be in the catalogue next to so many writing teachers I admire.

Thank you to my editor, Scott Francis, for his terrific input and help at every phase in the process.

Thank you to James Scott Bell for his excellent foreword, and to Donald Maas for his kind endorsement on the cover.

And thank you to the writers out there who love fiction and desire to do it well.

TABLE OF CONTENTS

FOREWORD

The night I murdered Jeff Gerke was also the night he was reani-
mated from the dead, just so he could write this book.

I trust my opening sentence has led you to this one. That's all
you have to do to write a hit novel, after all. String enough sentences together that compel the reader to read on and on until the
end, and then you're done.

Simple, isn't it? Sure, like climbing Mount Everest is simple.

But you can eventually scale the highest peak on the planet
with enough training and stamina, and by remembering that the
whole ascension starts with the first few steps. Just as writing a
great book begins with the first fifty pages.

Which is where Jeff Gerke comes in.

Jeff is an author himself (see the novels of Jefferson Scott) but
also an editor and publisher. He has therefore seen first pages from
all angles and knows whereof he speaks. He speaks clearly in this
book on the subject of how to write that crucial opening material.

You see, you really only have two choices: capture the reader
(or agent, or editor) in those first fifty pages or . . . don't.

Which do you choose?

I thought so. Jeff's book is here to help you. He'll show you
how it's done (and not done) so you can start up the mountain
with confidence.

Begin.

—James Scott Bell

❧ INTRODUCTION ❧

SUCH A YOUNG MAN.

Bushy hair. Narrow shoulders. A thin man. A little nerdy, even. Hardly the sort of leading man we expect today.

He looked almost shy as he thanked everyone who had spoken before him that day. He stared at the ground or his shoes or the notes before him. His opening lines were awkward, promising a tedious, interminable speech on a sweltering day under the Houston sun. He fumbled with the lectern while delivering a line with the unfortunate rhyming of *knowledge* and *college.*

But when he started his speech in earnest, the magic began.

"We set sail on this new sea because there is new knowledge to be gained," he said. Knowledge that "must be won and used for the progress of all people. ... There is no strife, no prejudice, no national conflict in outer space as yet. Its hazards are hostile to us all. Its conquest deserves the best of all mankind."

It was September 12, 1962, and John F. Kennedy was standing in Rice University stadium delivering what became perhaps his most famous speech. With his words and with the force of his will he was launching the U.S. space program, with the goal of putting an American astronaut on the moon before the end of the decade.

"'But why,' some say, 'choose the moon?'" he asked rhetorically. "'Why choose this as our goal?' And they might well ask, 'Why climb the highest mountain? Why, thirty-five years ago, fly the Atlantic? Why does Rice play Texas?'"

This got the laugh it deserved. Rice was known as a school for intellectuals, and their football team was routinely slaughtered by football powerhouse The University of Texas. But Jack raised his voice and cut through their laughter, uttering the lines that give me chills even today.

"We choose to go to the moon in this decade and do the other things—not because they are easy, but because they are hard."

Now their laughter turned to cheers. He rode their joy and turned it into an uproar.

"Because *that* goal will serve to organize and measure the best of our energies and skills. Because *that* challenge is one that we're willing to accept. One we are unwilling to postpone. And one we intend to win."

The goofy young man with the strange accent and the unruly hair had, with deft interplay of words and elements, generated a palpable energy in his listeners. An energy that had existed in potential form but had remained only latent until he began.

If he had asked that crowd to personally fund the mission to the moon at that very moment, I believe they would've done it. They would've found a way. John F. Kennedy ignited a movement that day, a force that swept up not only his hearers but the nation and the world, and we are still reaping the energy of his vision to this day.

Such is the power of a strong beginning.

❧ WE CHOOSE TO GO TO THE MOON ❧

The words you deploy in the first pages of your novel can and must have a similar power. They must arrest the imagination of your reader and fire his vision so he will go with you through the trials and triumphs of your story. You want him right with you to, in JFK's words, feel the ground shake and the air shatter by the sheer force of your tale as if it is the greatest adventure on which man has ever embarked.

You want your novel's launch to be as thrilling as the liftoff of a Saturn C-1 booster rocket. Whether it's an adventure story, a horror novel, a romantic comedy, a cozy mystery, or whatever else, you know your beginning must be strong, or the reader will never endure it long enough to get to the heart of your story.

You may already know a bit about how the publishing process works. You know that a literary agent or an acquisitions editor at a publishing house will decide the fate of your book based merely on its opening pages.

If you knew how little of a manuscript is read before a publisher chooses to accept or reject a book, you might be appalled. Usually it is only one person, the acquisitions editor, who has read the book from start to finish before a contract is offered—or not. All the other eight or twelve executives have read perhaps only fifty pages of the book. The *first* fifty pages. Or fewer. Maybe only the first ten. They trust the editor for the rest.

Most large publishing houses are closed to so-called *unsolicited submissions* (manuscripts not sent to them by agents). So, before your book's opening pages receive the scrutiny of a publishing house's executive committee, they must pass muster by a literary agent.

Agents receive thousands of manuscripts every year. Some receive tens of thousands. In an environment like that, it's simply human nature that they look for ways to quickly get through one proposal and get on to the next so they can reduce the slush pile at least a little.

Many of their rejections come easily: The author has not followed the agency's writer's guidelines or has sent a nonfiction proposal to an agent who accepts only fiction. But even with those eliminated, the stack of remaining manuscripts towers as high as a rocket on the launch pad.

Some agents will read a proposal in the order it's presented: cover letter, one-sheet, synopsis, etc., and then head to the sample chapters. Others—the fiction-lovers, mainly—will skip everything else and turn directly to page 1 of the chapters.

At that point, you've got about ten seconds to hook this person. Remember, she's looking for a reason to say no. Not because she's an ogre, but because she's in a hurry. She loves fiction, and she wants to love your book, and she must find new authors to keep her own business going, but there are so many others waiting in line—most of them, she knows, will end up being klunkers—that your book already has two strikes against it by the time she gets to page 1.

So your page 1 had better rock.

If your opening line manages to not offend her fiction sensibilities, and if your opening paragraphs keep her with you, she'll turn to page 2. With these early pages, you're basically in a moment-by-moment effort to skirt disaster with the agent or acquisitions editor. Disaster being the rejection of your manuscript. If you lose her in those early pages, you've lost her permanently.

It's like poor Westley in *The Princess Bride*. Every evening, his captor, the Dread Pirate Roberts, would send him to bed like this:

"Good night, Westley. Good work. Sleep well. I'll most likely kill you in the morning." With every line, paragraph, and page, the agent or editor is most likely going to kill your book in the morning. It is your task to "stay alive" as long as possible. To the very end, if you can, because that's where glory awaits.

It's not only agents and editors whom you must keep on the good side of. The same is true of your reader. You're trying to keep a very busy person from doing one of the hundred things he *ought* to be doing—or one of the many TV shows he wants to be watching—so he will read your book to the end. Enough missteps and the spell will be broken, and something else will capture his attention.

Years ago, I was looking for a new novel to read. So I went to the library and plucked off the new releases shelf ten books that looked interesting. I took them all to a table and opened them one by one. I was looking to be engaged. Hooked. Arrested by how the book began. Most of them failed utterly. They began with backstory, exposition, or something else utterly dull. Or their language was obtuse, showy, or any of a hundred other things that soured the book for me.

Granted, much of that is subjective, and there's no way you can anticipate and please every reader. But the point was that I was a reader wanting to be hooked by the novel's opening, and most of them botched it. So I put them all back on the shelf and went home with the one that grabbed me.

What is your situation? Have you been told that your openings tend to be weak? Do you sense that your whole book has gone wrong, and you have a hunch that it got off course at the outset? Are you paralyzed because you want to start your novel off right but you don't know how? Or maybe you're hoping this book will write the opening for you.

I'm like that. As I was writing this book, I was also in the midst of changing how I ran the accounting for the small indie press I founded. I'd been running it off a spreadsheet, but after our first two years the thing had just gotten to be unwieldy. It took me a week every time I had to figure royalties or pay taxes. It was aggravating. So at the recommendation of counselors I decided to transition from a spreadsheet to a database. (Don't let your eyes glaze over—I really am heading to a point!)

I purchased a very good database program and began figuring out how to run my publishing company from it. It wasn't long before I ended up in a terrible fix. I had tapped none of the strengths of the database and couldn't figure out how to do any of the things in a database that the spreadsheet program had done so easily. I'd lost way too much time in the effort, and I was now forced to run the business on both a database *and* the old spreadsheet. It was maddening.

So I did what any sensible person would do: I went online to Amazon.com! I found a terrific book on how to master the database program I was using. I read all the reviews and decided to take the plunge—even cashing in an Amazon gift card to do it.

Anxiously, I waited by the mailbox. When would the magical book come and solve all my problems? I could hold on until then, couldn't I?

Finally, it came! I ripped open the smiley face box and pulled out the talisman. It was indeed a tome. Half the weight of my toddler daughter, I reckoned. Surely the answers were here. I was saved!

I set it on my desk before my computer monitor, and waited. And waited.

Slowly it dawned on me that I might have all the answers before me, but the book wasn't going to solve my problems all by itself. I was going to have to open that beast and actually read it. *Read it?* It was 1,300 pages long, for crying out loud! And a bonus CD with 600 more pages! What had I been thinking? Where is my trusty spreadsheet?

[*bangs head on desk*]

My, we've come a long way from JFK to head-banging, haven't we? And in such a short time.

Anyway, I am saddened to inform you that, wonderful as this book may be, it will not write your first fifty pages for you.

However, if I do my job right, this book will energize you with all the electricity of a stirring speech, and you will ride the surge of inspiration all the way through those opening pages—and beyond. Because *we choose to go to the moon.* Not because it is easy, but because it is hard. And because, as Eugene F. Ware said, "All glory comes from daring to begin."

❧ IN THE BEGINNING WAS THE WORD ❧

Your novel can have a tremendous launch—not just so agents and editors will keep reading and not even so readers will stay with you, but so it will be strong as a work of literature. Structurally, the first fifty pages your of book have to accomplish certain objectives, or the foundation will be weak.

You have to engage your reader, first and foremost. You have to introduce your hero. You have to establish the context of the story. You must reveal the genre and milieu and story world. You have to set up the tone of the book. You'll also be presenting the stakes, introducing the antagonist, establishing the hero's desires, starting the main character's inner journey, and getting a ticking time bomb to start ticking down.

And you want to do all these things without boring your reader, losing your reader, dumping backstory on your reader, misleading your reader, insulting your reader's intelligence, or tipping your hand to your reader.

The first fifty pages of your book are so important to get right that it's tempting to say they are the *most* important pages in the manuscript. And yet they are, in a sense, merely the front work you have to do to get to the real heart of your story, which takes place in Act 2.

I recently bought my first Kindle e-reader. The box it came in was itself the beginning of a story—the tear-off strip for getting inside the box actually said "Once upon a time …" on it. As I lifted the lid and beheld the masterful presentation of the device so lovingly nestled inside, I felt the thrill of beginning a novel I just knew I was going to love. It was an undiscovered country, terra incognita, yet afire with possibilities.

That's the effect I'm going to teach you to achieve with the first fifty pages of your novel.

❧· WHO IS THIS PERSON? ·❧

Some readers don't feel a curiosity about who has written a given nonfiction book—they just want to get to the good stuff inside. I'm that way sometimes, depending on the book. Other times, I want to know who this person is who thinks he has something to teach me on this subject. In case that's how you're feeling this time, I offer a brief introduction to Jeff Gerke.

I entered the publishing industry in 1994, when I received a three-book deal to write a series of near-future technothrillers. I have now had six of my novels published (under the pen name Jefferson Scott), plus another six or so nonfiction books on a variety of topics, including three on fiction craftsmanship.

I have worked as a staff editor for three publishing companies and have done freelance editing and writing work for dozens of others. Of particular interest to the reader of this book, I have served as an acquisitions editor at those houses. That means I've read thousands and thousands of *first fifty pages*.

Books I have selected—based partially on those first pages—have won many major awards in my publishing category, including several Book of the Year awards. And I was recently a finalist for Editor of the Year for fiction in my industry niche.

In 2008 I launched my own small publishing company, Marcher Lord Press, which publishes science fiction and fantasy novels with a spiritual edge.

I am a regular faculty member at multiple writers conferences around the United States. Whether it's in the conference setting or in private coaching, I love helping novelists learn to better do what it is they're trying to do.

This led to my Fiction Writing Tip of the Week column (which is still available for free at www.WhereTheMapEnds.com), and all my fiction how-to books, including the Writer's Digest title *Plot Versus Character: A Balanced Approach to Writing Great Fiction.*

I have been told that one of my most valuable skills is the ability to diagnose what's working in a novel and what needs to be fixed—and exactly how to fix it.

That's the passion I bring to this book. I hope to use whatever clarity I can muster to help you see precisely how to structure your first fifty pages so they take off cleanly and expertly put your story "in orbit" for the reader's enjoyment.

⚜• PREFLIGHT CHECK •⚜

The First 50 Pages is divided into two parts. Part one gets you inside the heads of the first people who will encounter your opening pages: acquisitions editors and literary agents. There, you'll find out what these people are thinking and what factors weigh upon them as they decide whether or not to pursue publication of your novel. Knowing what they're dealing with will help you position your book for success.

In part two you'll get the full explanation of what your novel's first fifty pages have to accomplish, and how exactly to pull it all off. The final chapter in the book talks about how to take what you've done in those opening pages and continue it through page 51 and beyond.

As you read this book, you'll find that I use movies as my examples, even more than novels. I do so unapologetically, though I realize you're here to learn how to write a novel. That's for three reasons. One, movies are a perfect distillation of storytelling. They are, like short stories, fiction in a hurry. With only 120 pages to work with in a screenplay—and with most of it white space—you've got to nail the essence of the necessary components of good story with efficiency and precision.

Second, movies are part of our common culture and are therefore more likely to be familiar to you than perhaps a novel might be. If you're not already acquainted with a movie I refer to, it would take just two hours of your life to become an expert on it. That can't happen with a novel (well, for most people and most novels).

Third, like a good beginning to a novel, using movies as examples does more than one thing. It teaches you how to write good fiction, but it also teaches you how to write good screenplays. I can't speak for you, but most of the novelists I've spoken with over the years—myself included—secretly hope their novels will be turned into movies. Why not make it easy on the producer by writing a novel that could easily be adapted for the screen? And why not learn how to structure solid beginnings for two forms of media at once?

So if I cite *Toy Story 3* more than *Anna Karenina,* you'll know why. (Plus I'm a film-school grad, so my mind runs ever to movies anyway.)

❧• LET'S LIGHT THIS CANDLE •❧

A novel with a terrific first fifty pages is a novel that is very likely to get published. It's not a guarantee, because some people can write a great "launch" but then lose their way or have no ability to land the plane. But it *is* virtually guaranteed that a novel with a weak first fifty pages will not get published.

At the end of his speech, with LBJ wiping sweat from his forehead in the background and the sun beating down overhead, John F. Kennedy delivered these words:

"Many years ago, the great British explorer George Mallory, who was to die on Mount Everest, was asked why did he want to climb it. He said, 'Because it is there.' Well, *space* is there. And we're going to climb it. And the moon and the planets are there, and new hopes for knowledge and peace are there."

Dear writer, your novel's beginning is there, and new horizons of wonder and joy await us. So let's start the countdown on this thing, shall we? Time for liftoff.

PART 1

THE SUBMISSION
PROCESS

The secret of getting ahead is getting started. The secret to getting started is breaking your complex overwhelming tasks into small manageable tasks and then starting on the first one. **—MARK TWAIN**

FOR THE NEXT THREE CHAPTERS, I'M GOING TO TAKE you inside the mind of an acquisitions editor. It's a frightening place, I assure you. And yet your novel's first fifty pages will most likely have to pass through such a mind if your book is to ever get published. So it is a dark cave we must explore.

Most authors on the "pre-published" side of publishing companies tend to see them as faceless blocs, mysterious monoliths inside which arcane processes are brought to bear on books, resulting in sometimes brilliant, sometimes baffling, publishing decisions. A riddle, wrapped in a mystery, inside an enigma.

The reality is that publishing companies are just like any other kind of company. They're filled with people pretty much like you who make more or less the same decisions you would make if you were in their place. The key isn't to decrypt some kind of alien thought process, but to simply understand what factors are weighing on the mind of the person looking at your first fifty pages.

The insight you gain here will help you better craft your novel's opening, because you will understand the arena in which those first pages will be fighting.

CHAPTER 1

IN (AND OUT OF) THE BEGINNING

In the beginning the universe was created. This made a lot of people very angry and has been widely regarded as a bad idea. **–DOUGLAS ADAMS**

BEFORE AN ACQUISITIONS EDITOR GETS TO YOUR FIRST fifty pages—before, indeed, she gets to your proposal at all—she is thinking about many other things.

First, she's incredibly busy, and has most likely not been allocated any extra time in which she is allowed to go off into a corner and read through the stack of proposals and manuscripts sent to her by agents or amassed through other means. The so-called slush pile. And yet she knows she must find new novels to fill the open slots in her upcoming release schedule, and she knows she has to find good new novels, both to help the company succeed in the future and to secure her own position in the publishing house. Editors at publishing companies tend to come and go as quickly as football coaches with losing teams. So she knows she has to score a few touchdowns for the team, and that involves finding good new books.

And by "good" I don't necessarily mean well written or literarily remarkable. I mean good in terms of sales. In publishing companies, editors are thought of as the brainiacs who sit in their ivory towers thinking lofty thoughts about Keats, Milton, and Shakespeare. They tend to love good writing—especially when it comes to fiction—and to value craftsmanship and the potential for literary contribution over plebian concerns such as making enough money from sales to keep the doors open and the lights on.

The second concern weighing on our underpaid and heroic acquisitions editor, therefore, is the question of whether or not any of the proposals in her slush pile could possibly make the publishing company a boatload of money. She's learned the hard way that she's not to be looking for Faulkners or Steinbecks or Forsters, but Benjamins. Cash cows. Books that will sell lots of copies and save the company for another six months.

Now, our heroine knows all this, but she still loves a great story and still values the work of a skilled wordsmith. So she resolves to find the best-written novels she can that will possibly turn a profit. She might in the end be pushed to acquire a book she finds terrible but that will undoubtedly sell well, but until that time comes, she is going to try to do both. When she's looking at your first fifty pages, she's hoping you will help her do this.

It would be nice to be able to publish the books an editor loves, without any regard for making money, but this does not usually happen. (Except in the world of indie publishing and micro-publishing like I do, but that's a topic for another book.)

The person looking at your first fifty pages is stressed, unsure about her own job security, overworked, burdened with the need to read proposals but allocated no time to do so, and trying to find novels that are both wonderfully written and financially viable.

Literary agents are looking for many of the same things that acquisitions editors look for, though their slush pile is much, much larger and of much poorer quality. The typical agent is open to anyone who can send him an e-mail, whereas the acquisitions editor at a large house is mostly shielded from this. The proposals she receives have been vetted by agents, who have gone through the *real* slush pile and discovered the most promising projects.

The best agents are those who have first been acquisitions editors, because that teaches them what their customers—the current acquisitions editors at publishing houses—are thinking and looking for. So when an agent reads your first fifty pages, he's probably busy, probably overworked, but probably not as concerned about job security. He may or may not be interested in fine writing, though he knows that some of his customers are, so he has gained some knowledge of what is considered good fiction craftsmanship, and he applies this knowledge as he searches the pile.

Mainly, an agent is looking for what projects could potentially be big sales hits. He knows that the editor he's going to pitch to is concerned about this, but mainly he knows how the game is played. He knows that it is the publisher's vice-presidents of sales and marketing, more than the monk-scholar editors, who are going to be most instrumental in making final publishing decisions. So he's thinking about the publishing committee ("PubCo") meetings yet in the future. When an agent reads your first fifty pages, he's thinking about the finish line.

And you thought publishing was just about companies putting out books you might like. There's a lot going on, but the mechanism is no black box. You just need to understand that publishing is a business. Well, it's actually more like gambling, but I'll stick with "business" for now.

❧· NOW FOR THE PROPOSAL ·❧

So you've gotten inside the head of an acquisitions editor. She has carved out some time to read through the pile—possibly by taking a bunch of proposals home with her over the weekend—and has given herself the goal of getting through one hundred of them before coming up for air. She's keeping in mind all the things we've talked about already, but she's really hoping to find a few gems. So she opens the first mailer or the first attachment on her e-mail and gets to work.

A fiction proposal has two main components: front matter and sample chapters. The front matter has a cover letter, various blurbs and hooks as the "sizzle," plus the author's bio and publishing credits, perhaps a marketing analysis of comparable books, and a one-page synopsis (the "steak"). The sample chapters contain the first contiguous thirty to fifty pages of the novel.

The first fifty pages.

As we've seen, some editors (and agents) will skip everything else and go right to the sample chapters. The front matter is vital, of course, and it's not a proper proposal without it, but the editor's focus is on your craftsmanship and your story.

But she's also trying to get through one hundred of these in a hurry. Yours is number sixty-two, and she's getting a little numb in the brain. She's found a couple of proposals that look interesting, and she's set these aside to contact the agents and request the full manuscripts. (Hint: a first-time author won't be taken seriously until the rough draft is finished, so don't even approach agents before yours is complete.)

Now she opens yours and starts reading. She's hoping it will be fantastic, but in her experience she knows the odds are against it.

There are a number of things she might see right away in your proposal that will get your book an instant *no*. Like a nonfiction proposal that has been sent to a house that publishes only fiction. Like a Satanic horror novel sent to a conservative Christian publisher. Like a proposal that does not follow the publisher's writer's guidelines. Like an unsolicited proposal sent uninvited. Like a men's adventure novel sent to a romance publisher. Most of these can be avoided by doing just fifteen minutes of research on any publisher (or agent) you target.

Then there are factors the editor is aware of but that you have no way of knowing. Like the fact that your romantic comedy about vampires in love is too similar to a book they're coming out with in the spring. Or how the sales department has just announced that they don't want to see another Amish novel for the next two years, and yours is an Amish novel. Or the fact that the publisher has given the editor a mandate not to come to him with anything but cyborg science fiction involving a drug that prolongs life indefinitely, and yours isn't anything like that.

There will always be unknowns affecting how your novel is received. You can't do anything about such things, so there's no point in worrying about them. You just concentrate on writing the best book you can—and, for the proposal, the best first fifty pages you can—and let the chips fall where they may.

But let's say your proposal has hurtled each of these obstacles and is still in play in the editor's mind. She likes your front matter and is ready to sink her teeth into your first fifty pages. Well, your first line, at least.

THE AGE OF SELF-PUBLISHING

It bears mentioning that what I've described so far refers to a model of publishing that may be passing away. Whether because of a long recession or because technology has brought about a new publishing paradigm, the old way is becoming rare. More and more small presses are cropping up, presses without a vice-president in sight.

And micro-publishing, niche publishing, and self-publishing are becoming more accepted.

With bookstores dying and publishers wanting to publish only surefire hits (read: books by authors who have recently written best-sellers), unpublished and even mid-list authors are beginning to ask, "Now, wait a minute—tell me again why I need a publisher?"

For decades, the bookstore/publisher dyad has been the power bloc that mandated what kinds of novels were published and what kinds were not. Now bookstores are dying, which has the consequence of causing many traditional publishers to decline. The old power bloc is fading, and writers who have their whole lives been marginalized—because they didn't write what was considered acceptable—are beginning to step out into the sun. It's a terrific time to be a novelist with a fresh approach or style or genre or story. We're in a publishing revolution right now, one that is so conducive to downtrodden fiction writers that I like to call it Revenge of the Writers.

Many authors are deciding to dispense with the traditional publishing model and try another route. I encourage such writers to do so. However, this new model has good and bad aspects. The one I want to mention is the lack of a vetting process.

If you self-publish, or if you go with a micro-press that gives very little expert editorial input, you won't have to worry about anything I've mentioned in this chapter. In such a scenario, your novel will be published no matter how good it is. You won't have to be concerned about agents or editors rejecting your proposal. It would be tempting for a person in that situation to forget about craft altogether—there's nothing about low craftsmanship or a poor first fifty pages that will bar your book from publication, so why worry?

You are obviously not like this, or you wouldn't have picked up this book. You are concerned about beginning your novel with all the loving craftsmanship you can summon. I applaud you.

Just know that others, particularly other novelists who have self-published, may not understand why you labor so hard on your first fifty pages or any other part of your book. You know, of course, but they may not get it. If you decide to self-publish or to go with a press that gives no true edit, I recommend you hire the services of a veteran fiction editor to give your novel a solid editorial pass.

I'm a big believer in niche publishing, since that's what my own publishing company does. But there has to be something more than external factors causing you to want to make your novel the best it can be. That's the kind of commitment to excellence that will set your work apart from the flash fiction around us and give it a chance at a long life.

❧• THE SAMPLE CHAPTERS •❧

An acquisitions editor (or agent) is, unfortunately, in a position to have to say no to most of the proposals she looks at. So, while she's eagerly hoping your chapters will be wonderful and your proposal is one she can love, she's expecting it not to be, and she's hoping it will show itself to be one or the other in the first few seconds she's going to give your book.

The First 50 Pages is all about what goes into a great beginning for a novel. But let's spend a minute talking about what does *not* belong in the beginning of a novel. If you want the editor to keep reading, avoid these pitfalls. In part two we'll talk about how to build a great beginning. But let's take a moment to talk about how to not build a bad one.

Over the years, and after tens of thousands of aromatic first pages, I have compiled a list of mistakes I've seen again and again. Reading about them in negative form will help you avoid these errors, and will also give you early insight into what *should* go into a good opening.

Some of these negatives we'll talk about in this chapter. The rest we'll discuss in positive form in later chapters.

I (and agents and editors across the publishing industry) have rejected fiction proposals for these reasons:

- Weak first line
- Starting with a dream scenario
- Lack of an engaging hook
- Telling instead of showing
- Point-of-view errors
- Shallow characters
- Lack of beats for pacing and description
- Stilted dialogue
- Clumsy fiction craftsmanship
- Inadequate descriptions of characters and settings (or details that are introduced to the reader too late)
- Starting the main action too soon
- Going into flashbacks too early in the story
- Jumping to a new viewpoint character too early
- Too little conflict
- Lack of stakes or a ticking time bomb

The acquisitions editor won't necessarily reject a book for one of these reasons alone. Just because a novel's first line is weak, for instance, doesn't necessarily mean the whole book is going to be terrible. Often, the better opening line is buried somewhere on page 1. That can be fixed in an edit. But pile up enough of these—even just two or three, especially if they're all in the first pages—and this book is going down.

In chapter two, we'll go through these one by one.

CHAPTER 2
PROPOSAL KILLERS

A bad beginning makes a bad ending. **–EURIPIDES**

I MENTIONED EARLIER THAT I AM A FREQUENT TEACHER at writers conferences. One of my classes has the unwieldy title "The Top Three Errors That Will Kill Your Fiction's Chances With Editors, and How to Eliminate Them (the Errors, Not the Editors)."

There are actually twenty errors I talk about in class. The top three are big enough that they're the topic of chapter three. But I'll go over the others here.

When we last left our intrepid acquisitions editor, she was sitting down to read your sample chapters. She's seen enough proposals in her career to be able to spot warning signs very quickly in those first pages.

In chapter one I gave a partial list of miscues she's hoping not to find but more or less expecting to see in your opening chapters. Now let's look at them one at a time.

❧ THE LA BREA TAR PITS ❧

A weak first line is a killer. You get only one first line, so make sure it's carefully thought-out. And please don't make it some form of "Jake got out of the car." Don't let anybody get out of a car in the first sentence of your book. I'm sort of joking, but it's such a cliché to start this way that some agents and editors actually *will* decline a book based on that.

Speaking of clichés, please don't start your novel with a dream. Authors often do this because of the notion that they should start with action—which is a good thing. But if how they'd planned to start the book is not active, they think they'll solve the problem by beginning with some dramatic scene that gets the reader engaged. And then the character wakes up and we realize it was all just a dream. It's a good way to aggravate your reader—and get your book rejected by an agent or editor.

Your opening lines must hook your reader. You must start with action. But that doesn't mean you have to have a battle scene or that anything needs to blow up. It simply means it must be interesting to the reader. It may be fascinating to you how the clouds billow high above the hero's city, or you may be eager to get the reader into the mental processes of the protagonist, but your novel has to start with something that will be interesting *to the reader*.

With this and many other topics in this book, it will behoove you to think of yourself not as a novelist but as a screenwriter. As you're contemplating how your novel should begin, think of it as a movie. If your proposed beginning were being watched by a theater audience, how would it play?

A long, still shot of clouds billowing? Boring. A person sitting there thinking? Snoozeville. Ah, but someone *doing something,* especially something interesting—even if it's just something unusual but not inherently captivating, like erecting a pup tent or tending a beehive—would be an engaging way for a movie, or a novel, to start.

I'm going to be talking about show vs. tell, point of view, and characters at length in the next chapter, so I'll skip those for now. Just know that those are the big three for how to kill your book's chances with editors and agents.

❦· BEATS ·❦

Beats are bits of narrative that occur during a dialogue exchange. For instance, here's a passage from *Water for Elephants* by Sara Gruen:

> "Oh, here," clucks Hazel. "Let's give Jacob a look."
>
> She pulls Dolly's wheelchair a few feet back and shuffles up beside me, clasping her hands, her milky eyes flashing. "Oh, it's so exciting! They've been at it all morning!"

The nondialogue sentence in this passage is a beat. This simple sentence accomplishes three things: It shows us what's happening "on-stage," it ties us to the setting of the scene, and it gives a buffer—a "beat" of silence, to use theatrical terms—between the two characters' lines of dialogue.

Without beats, your dialogue scenes feel rushed and clumsy, and they become detached from the setting and begin to be talking heads floating away into the stratosphere. Consider this exchange from *König's Fire* by Marc Schooley without any of its beats:

> "Nice to meet you, Gott. I think we can dispense with all the formalities down here in this hole."
>
> "You're different from our last Oberleutnant."
>
> "In what way?"
>
> "I never shook hands with an officer before."
>
> "I doubt you're any more of a man for having done so. What's with the face here?"
>
> "Permission to speak freely, sir?"

"Natürlich."

"I doubt I'm any *less* of a man for it, either."

"Perhaps not, Obergrenadier. What kind of Nazi are you, with black hair and eyes?"

"Nazis are not as they look but as they do, sir. We leave this one alone, sir. It'll cloud your mind if you look at it too much. We never touch it."

How did that read to you? Some pretty good dialogue, but doesn't it feel hurried? Don't the lines of dialogue feel like they've been shot out of a machine gun? Did you feel you knew where you were or what the characters were doing, besides talking? And you're probably a little lost and feeling like you've missed some of what's going on, especially at the end.

That's because the beats are missing.

Here it is with the beats restored:

"Nice to meet you, Gott. I think we can dispense with all the formalities down here in this hole." I stuck my hand out to shake.

Gott seemed to make sure I had not offered him the hand that recently was affixed to the granite, and then he shook. His hand was soft, but the grip was firm. "You're different from our last Oberleutnant."

"In what way?"

"I never shook hands with an officer before."

"I doubt you're any more of a man for having done so," I said. "What's with the face here?"

"Permission to speak freely, sir?"

I nodded. "Natürlich."

"I doubt I'm any *less* of a man for it, either." Gott strained his eyes at me through the thick glasses. It was clear to me he was studying me, quickly and intently, though it looked like he was doing it through a fish tank. I wondered if we ever see anyone more closely than that, no matter if we wear glasses or not.

"Perhaps not, Obergrenadier," I said. "What kind of Nazi are you, with black hair and eyes?" I studied Gott's reaction. Two could dance this dance.

"Nazis are not as they look but as they do, sir." His eyes did not flinch behind the glasses. He turned and pointed at the granite face. "We leave this one alone, sir. It'll cloud your mind if you look at it too much. We never touch it."

Makes a little more sense now, doesn't it? Did you notice how the beats varied the rhythm of the spoken dialogue? A beat implies a pause. If you want to imply a long pause in your dialogue, write a long beat. Short beats equal short pauses.

Notice also that the beats tethered you to the setting. They showed you what was going on in the scene and where characters were in relation to one another. If dialogue is the audio track, beats are the video track.

Beats give us the viewpoint character's thoughts and perceptions, too, as when the character noticed that Gott's hands were soft but his grip was firm.

Beats are your friends. Use them, and your book's opening will begin to take on the texture of mastery.

❧ STILTED DIALOGUE ❧

This isn't a book on how to write dialogue. However, I mention it because poor dialogue is something you must not have in your first fifty pages if you want agents and editors to keep reading and not toss your proposal on the reject stack. I know editors who will skip everything else in a proposal, go straight to the first section of dialogue they can find, and begin reading.

In order for dialogue to work in a novel, it must be realistic, layered, and *right* for the character and the moment.

Unrealistic dialogue is what I like to call dialogue that is *on the nose*:

> "My, Jenny, you are looking chipper today."
>
> "Yes, Charles, I am chipper. And would you like to know why?"
>
> "Yes, I would like to know why you are chipper today. Please tell me."
>
> "Thank you. I will tell you. I am chipper because of my aunt."
>
> "Your aunt? How does your aunt make you chipper?"
>
> "Oh, Charles, you are silly. My aunt makes me chipper because she is here."
>
> "I am not silly. And I did not know your aunt was here."

Blah, blah, blah. One of the (many) possible forms of unrealistic dialogue is dialogue in which characters politely take turns and answer exactly what each other says, like Charles and Jenny. A more realistic exchange would go something like this:

> "My, Jenny, you're looking chipper today."
>
> "Oh, yeah? Hmm. I guess it's because of my aunt."
>
> Charles's forehead wrinkled. "Wait, your Aunt Gillespie?"
>
> "Nope. Charles, Aunt Gillespie's been dead two years."
>
> "Oh."
>
> She shrugged. "Anyway, it's my Aunt Elaine. It always cheers me up when she comes."
>
> "How so?"

It's still not an exchange that is going to make it into a book about stellar dialogue, but at least it feels more realistic.

Good dialogue is also layered. In theater, it's called *subtext*. Actors learn not only their lines, but the intent behind the lines. One benefit of this is that if they forget the actual lines when they're onstage, they'll be able to ad lib something that amounts to the same thing.

In good dialogue, dialogue with subtext, the characters aren't responding to what the other person says, but to what they think the other person *means*:

> "My, Jenny, you're looking chipper today."
>
> She growled. "I haven't been drinking, all right?"
>
> Charles looked surprised. "Hey, I wasn't going to bring it up. But since you did ..."
>
> "My, Charles," Jenny said in a mocking tone, "you're looking less stupid today."
>
> He laughed. "At least stupid is something you're born with."
>
> She spun to him. "As opposed to what?"
>
> "You know."

Or whatever. Dialogue like this feels realistic. When was the last time someone said something to you like, "Looks like you got a lot accomplished today" and you didn't think *What is she really saying?* Give your dialogue subtext, and it will be easier for agents and editors—and readers—to love your novel.

Finally, be sure your dialogue is *right* for your character and right for the moment. One of the surest ways to show you may not be ready for prime time as a novelist is if your characters feel shallow and undifferentiated. More about that in the next chapter, but for now just understand that characters speak differently based on who they are and what situation they find themselves in.

"Mm. Help you, I can."

Can you identify that character? (It's Yoda from the *Star Wars* movies.) How he speaks identifies him. Now, you don't have to invent a new syntax for each of your characters. But if Yoda suddenly went from "How you get so big, eating food of this kind?" to "Excuse me, darling, but your chapeau has been left on the divan," you'd blow your reader's believability in your characters and his faith in your writing. Make sure your characters' dialogue is right for who they are.

Also, be sure your characters' dialogue is right for the moment. If you've got two characters swimming out to sea to rescue someone, their conversation shouldn't look like this:

> "Now, Thomas, when we approach the swimmer, we must do so with extreme caution. I shall attempt to maneuver behind him and affix my arms about him in a forceful, decisive manner to communicate that I am taking the lead in the moment."
>
> "Very well then, Sebastian. I shall observe and assist as necessary."

To seem real, it would probably go something more like this:

> "Stay back," Sebastian said, spitting out seawater. "I'm gonna ... get behind ... grab him."
>
> "What?"
>
> "Got to be ... firm." He gasped heavily.
>
> Thomas wondered if Sebastian had the strength for this. "You sure?"
>
> "Yeah. Got to show him ... who's in charge."
>
> "Okay, good. I'm here."

Great dialogue may not get you a publishing contract, but lousy dialogue will often prevent you from getting one. Awkward, unrealistic dialogue is a common reason acquisitions editors and agents will decline the opportunity to publish your novel.

❧• CLUMSY FICTION CRAFTSMANSHIP •❧

This is a broad category. It involves a number of minor technique failures that, by themselves, don't mean much but that usually go along with an underdeveloped fiction skill-set. It includes things that are subjective to some degree or that vary from editor to editor and agent to agent. But if they appear in your first fifty pages, they can nevertheless get your book rejected.

For instance, I personally have a problem with sentences that begin with participial phrases, especially those that have nothing to do with what comes after.

> Having grown up in Louisiana, Kim decided to have a sandwich.

> Collecting Beanie Babies all through his college years, John was left-handed.

This usually comes from a writer trying to do too much with a single sentence. He feels he must get all this information in, but he doesn't want to devote too much time to giving it, so he cobbles together two (or more) elements and joins them with a comma.

Seeing too many participial phrases in the first fifty pages, the editor declined the book.

Another example of clumsy writing, in my opinion anyway, is the use of speech attributions other than *said* or *asked*.

> "Why, yes," he harrumphed.
> "You didn't," she breathed.
> "No!" he lurched.
> "But why?" she inquired.
> "Perhaps it was your bad manners," he opined.
> "It can't be," she sighed.
> "You crack me up," he laughed.
> "Stop it now!" he barked.
> "What a ham," she smiled.

Or some of my favorites:

> "Yes," he agreed.
> "I'm sorry," she apologized.

Aaaaagh! Stop the madness!

Now, I know why authors do this. On the whole, we are taught to use variety in our prose and eschew pet phrases or overused words. All well and good. But when it comes to speech attributions, you want to be invisible. You want to draw attention to the characters' speech, not to your clever vocabulary.

There is a small pool of speech attributions that are invisible to the reader. They are said, asked, shouted, whispered, and muttered. Maybe half a dozen others.

Notice that they all have in common the fact that they are all actions that allow for the delivery of actual speech. Have you ever tried to growl out a line of dialogue? Go on, try it. You can't. You can either growl or you can speak, but you can't do both at the same time. What about laughing out audible words? Hissing them out? Smiling your words?

Even some words that allow speech should be avoided, like uttered, sermonized, and insulted. They're just obtrusive, and chances are that the insult, to pick one, is inherent in the content of the thing spoken. Just write, "'You dork,' he said," and give the reader the benefit of the doubt that she'll understand it was an insult.

Clumsy fiction technique is something the acquisitions editor is watching for. She may not even know all the names for it, but she knows it when it's there. To be sure your book doesn't have these, there's nothing to do but simply keep improving your craft. As you elevate your skill level in the biggies, like the things I cover in chapter three, these niggling things tend to take care of themselves.

❧· DESCRIPTION ·❧

There is a school of thought in fiction that says the author ought not describe anything or anyone in the book. "Let the reader see my places and people as he will," is the refrain. "I will never dictate anything for the reader."

I am not of this school.

In my opinion, this choice not to describe is often a decision stemming less from artistic laissez-faire and more from simple laziness. It takes a great burden off the author not to have to decide what anyone or anything looks like, much less to convey that to the reader. But it leaves the reader adrift and makes the characters seem faceless and the places seem like formless nebulae.

This isn't the place to go into detail about how to write satisfactory description, but I would urge you to go to every new setting and character in your book and, when introducing them at least, consider how you might describe them. Can you add sensory details? How about comparisons ("A room the size of a racquetball court"), word pictures ("He looked like a skinny Elvis"), or definitive details? Look for opportunities to describe the lighting, the weather, and the number and relative position of the players onstage.

For characters, describe them as soon as they step onstage the first time. Rather, describe them as soon as the viewpoint character notices them the first time, because that's when the reader wants to know what they look like. For settings, you should have begun describing them by the end of the first page of a scene in a new location.

If I'm reading an author's first pages and I can't picture the places or people, I stop reading. And so do many acquisitions editors and agents.

❧· TOO EARLY OR TOO LITTLE ·❧

A novel can be rejected if the author has done some things too early or other things not enough. I discuss these in positive form in the following chapters, so I'll just breeze over them here.

A common mistake is to begin the main action of the story on page 1. In the first few paragraphs, the *Titanic* hits the iceberg or the *Hindenburg* catches fire or the love interest announces she's moving away. We don't care about anyone in the story yet, so dropping the big bomb on page 1 has less than no dramatic effect.

I'm not a fan of flashbacks or frame devices (in which a short scene in one era brackets the whole rest of the story, which is told in flashback), but that's largely subjective. Even so, launching too quickly into a time other than the one you start with is also a mistake. The reader hasn't gotten her bearings in the first era yet, and she certainly can't hang with you if you make a jump in time right away.

Some novelists introduce too many viewpoint characters too early. On page 1 we meet Virginia, who longs to get into the USC Film School. On page 1.5 we meet Jerome, who is in year seventeen of his missionary work in Peru. On page 2 we meet Cho, who still lives at home in Szechuan, though her parents want her to move out. On page 2.75 we meet Opal, who can't afford her medication. And so it goes, with new characters and story lines introduced bang-bang-bang, one after another. It's like watching TV with someone who has ADD—and the remote.

Authors do this because they want to show how interesting their book will be and how epic in scope it is. But it's a mistake. Readers don't really know who Virginia is yet, but on you go to Jerome. You ask your readers to stop caring about her and begin caring about him. In the name of reader engagement, you actually prevent your readers from engaging at all.

Editors and agents know to look for these things. If you introduce elements in your first fifty (or ten) pages that shouldn't be introduced until later, if at all, your book may get rejected.

It's also possible to do too little of some things in your opening pages.

Too little conflict, for instance. If your first pages make it seem that the book is going to be about the wonders of what will grow in someone's new flower bed, you're going to get a rejection. If the novel's first pages seem to be introducing a book about the great sit-in for peace of 1972, you may be out of luck. Fiction is conflict: someone who wants something but is prevented from getting it. Without it, your book will probably not get published. The acquisitions editor is looking for signs of conflict in your first fifty pages.

An absence of stakes or suspense in your first pages is something else that will spell trouble for your book. If there is nothing at stake (that the reader cares about), you have no reader buy-in. So if the beginning has your hero racing home to get to the party in time because, if he doesn't, he … will just be a little late, it's a snoozer, and it will likely be rejected.

❧· ON "DON'TS" AND "DOS" ·❧

You may have noticed that each of these don'ts is really a do turned backward. You *do* want to describe your settings adequately. You *do* want to include realistic dialogue. You *do* want to use beats to manage the rhythm and pacing of your dialogue scenes. I look at these in positive form in the body of this book. But I hope it's been helpful to see them as mines to avoid stepping on.

Now for the big three—the three main errors that will kill your fiction's chances with editors—and how to eliminate them. The errors, not the editors.

CHAPTER 3

THREE BOMBS

The beginning is the most important part of any work, especially in the case of a young and tender thing; for that is the time at which the character is being formed and the desired impression is more readily taken. —PLATO

FOR ONE MORE CHAPTER WE'RE GOING TO BE INSIDE the recesses of an acquisitions editor's or agent's mind. Our topic here is the three main craft errors that most often cause agents and acquisitions editors to reject fiction proposals. If one or more of these errors appear to any great degree in the first fifty pages, the book will most likely be declined.

That's not to say that every editor rejects books because of these things, or that lots of novels don't get published with these errors in abundance. But most editors and agents, if they love fiction craftsmanship and they have their druthers, will decline books that evidence these fiction blunders.

The big three bombs are telling instead of showing, point-of-view errors, and weak characters. Other publishing professionals might add to my list or replace one or more items with others, but it's about as close to a consensus list as you're going to find.

This is not a book on general fiction craftsmanship, so I won't be going into as much detail on these subjects as I could. Indeed, entire books have been written on each topic. Laurie Alberts wrote a book called *Showing & Telling,* for instance. Alicia Rasley has *The Power of Point of View.* And for character development, I've written *Plot Versus Character,* also published by Writer's Digest Books.

Here, I'm just going to give you "the skinny" on each of these topics, why they will diminish your chances of getting published, and how to overcome them.

❧• SHOW VS. TELL •❧

Showing and telling is an aspect of fiction craftsmanship that at first defies common sense. When we are having a polite conversation with someone, we know we must first inform the listener of certain key details or the listener will be lost when we tell the story.

If I were to tell you "The answer is seven," you would have no clue what I was talking about. But if I were to have first said, "I watched *Snow White* the other day. Can you tell me how many dwarves there were in the story?" you would certainly know what I was talking about when I then said, "The answer is seven."

In polite conversation—and in nearly all nonfiction forms of communication, be it a speech, a how-to book, or an e-mail—you must provide the recipient with a quantity of information before she can comprehend what you're going to say next. We first provide the *context* of what is to follow. To not do so is to fail to communicate clearly, which is something we writers strive heartily to avoid.

So it makes perfect sense that a novelist would sit down and fill the first ten to thirty pages of his novel with explanation. With context. We don't want our reader to be confused, after all. When our reader encounters something in our story, we want her to have been pre-informed about it so it won't trip her up as she reads.

Thus we get novels that start with the history of civilization. Or perhaps how the hero's parents met. Or the heroine's life story. Or

THE FIRST 50 PAGES

the high points of the founding and development of the corporation that is going to form the backdrop for most of the book.

In fiction, this kind of information dumping is called *telling*. Its main forms are backstory, pure exposition, summary/recap, and the explanation of character motives. We can clearly see why authors do this. They are, after all, merely following the rules of polite conversation that apply to almost every other area of discourse.

The problem is that it makes for terrible fiction.

Confession time: I'm a science fiction geek. I own and have watched the 5-disc Blu-Ray version of *Blade Runner*. I was watching *Dangerous Days,* the documentary about the making of *Blade Runner,* when I came upon an awesome quotation from Harrison Ford talking about, of all things, show vs. tell:

> There was a voice-over narration attached to the original script, and I said to Ridley [Scott, the director] that I played a detective who does no detecting. How about we take some of this information that's in the voice-overs and put it into scenes, so that the audience could discover the information, discover the character through seeing him in the context of what he does, rather than being told about it.

Even the actors get it! When you load your story with telling, you deprive your reader—and even your characters—of the joy of having it all happen experientially. Take the information out of the voice-overs (your telling) and put it into scenes. Thank you, Mr. Ford.

Since I've brought up a movie, let's go back to our filmmaker metaphor. I want you to no longer think of yourself as a straight storyteller, but as someone making a movie. Here, as in so many areas of fiction, thinking in terms of cinema will automatically improve your novel.

How do you think a movie would fare at the box office if its first ten minutes consisted of a black screen over which a narrator recounted the history of the world?

Can you just see it? All the people sitting there in the dark, looking in vain at a screen that gives them no images, having to force their minds to concentrate on a lecture about ancient history? It would never work. The movie would fail miserably in its first week in theaters.

All because of a botched beginning.

A novel that begins with telling has the same effect on a reader (and an acquisitions editor or agent) as that movie would have on a viewer. You've got to make things happen in front of the reader's eyes. You've got to bring things onstage and have more than narration alone. You have to, in filmmaking terms, place something in front of the camera.

We're not just having a polite conversation here—we're making a movie (in book form). This isn't the time to explain everything first; it's the time to start the camera to rolling and watch events unfold.

How do movies begin? With something interesting happening onscreen. Do they explain everything first? Do they say, "Okay, this girl used to live in Lincoln but now she's moved to Pasadena to try to make it as an actress," or do they just … start? Do they *show* her going to auditions or digging through her glove compartment past old maps of Nebraska to find her map of the stars?

Telling is static information-dumping. It's boring. It makes your reader's eyes glaze over and it turns his brain off. Trust me, this is not the effect you want your first fifty pages to have on your reader, especially if that reader has the power to get your book published.

Here's my definition of telling: *Telling is when you stop the story to explain something the reader doesn't care about.*

As you're thinking about how to begin your novel, don't worry about what you feel you should explain first so the reader won't be lost. Think instead what would be a cool—and very visual—way to begin your movie ... er, novel. In a minute, I'll teach you ways to reveal information through *showing* while still advancing the story and revealing characters. But for now, just think less about explaining and more about engaging. Everything the reader needs to know can come out later and be revealed in natural ways. Don't sink your novel by loading it down with exposition. Get on with the fun.

RULE OF THUMB

I'll give you a little tool here that could revolutionize your understanding of showing and telling in fiction. I may not be the first person to talk about it in these terms, but I know I'd never heard it before I thought it up. So I'm at least its co-inventor.

Maybe you want to rid your fiction of telling but you simply can't see it—not in other people's fiction and certainly not in your own. So how can you delete something you can't even see?

There's a question you can ask of any passage you feel may be telling. You ready?

Get the passage in front of you and ask this of it: *Can the camera see it?*

There are exceptions, but *Can the camera see it?* is a terrific tool for helping you begin to see the telling in a manuscript.

Let's test it:

> Kinkaide had always loved flowers. Even when he was a child, he
> would work for hours in the sun digging in the garden and plant-

ing his flowers, which usually ended up being weeds. But he loved it and grew up hoping to become a horticulturalist.

Okay, now load up the testing gun and fire: Can the camera see this? If this were a movie, what would be on the screen during this part? Which elements of what is written here can be seen by a camera (and we're not talking about a flashback)?

Answer: none. The camera can't see it because it's nothing but *telling.*

Let's look at another:

> Urlandia was a peaceful realm. Peasants and nobles alike lived in harmony despite the occasional bout with famine or invaders from the neighboring kingdom of Dûm. There were heroes and cads, pirates and tavern wenches, and in all, their lives were good.

Okay, aside from this being deadly dull, is it showing or telling? Let's load up the testing gun and fire: Can the camera see it?

Your mind might have conjured up an image of a fantasy countryside with green meadows, vast forests, and castles with pennants flapping in the breeze, but how could you have seen "the occasional bout with famine"? How could you see that the invaders were from the neighboring kingdom of Dûm? How could you see that their lives were good? You couldn't. You weren't shown any of this—you were simply told. And it probably left you feeling a little sleepy.

It would be quite possible to convert this telling to showing by depicting things *before the camera's lens* that suggest each of these elements. But right now it's unconverted telling.

I can't tell you how many unpublished novels I've seen that start like this. And I've rejected every single one of them. You don't want your book rejected, so don't put telling anywhere in the first fifty pages.

One more:

> Veronica shifted into park and got out of her VW bug. She shield-
> ed her eyes from the afternoon sun and stared at the house.
> It was smaller than she remembered. And had it always been
> this run-down, or had it fallen into disrepair only lately? It had
> once been white, but the siding slats desperately needed a
> new paint job.
>
> Two giant antennae poked up from the roof like alien ten-
> tacles. They were held in place by cables, but the one on the
> right nevertheless tilted at a diagonal. Maybe it helped with re-
> ception. The porch was covered by an awning of flaking wood.
> Whether the walls beneath the awning were worse off than the
> rest or they just looked that way because they were shrouded in
> shadow, Veronica couldn't tell.
>
> She sighed. If this is where she came from, no wonder she'd
> turned out as she had.

Okay, load up the testing gun. Can the camera see this?

Actually, yes.

Aside from a violation of the rule not to start a novel with someone getting out of a car, it's not terrible prose. It's description. Some
people would be inclined to cut it because nothing seems to be happening: It's neither action nor dialogue, so it must be telling. But
that would be a mistake. As we saw in chapter two, a lack of description can get your book declined. Description isn't telling because ...
the camera can see it. Without description, the reader can't visual-
ize the story—which means that your story can't go forward without description. Don't leave it out.

As I mentioned, there are exceptions. The camera can't see
sounds or smells or temperatures or tastes, though a description
of those things would not be telling. Also, interior monologue—
the viewpoint character's thoughts and interpretations—can't be

seen by a camera and is therefore not (usually) telling. But on the whole, *Can the camera see it?* will help you immediately spot and eliminate telling.

EXCEPTIONS AND SPECIAL CATEGORIES

Is telling ever okay in a novel? Yes, but not in the first fifty pages of your book. And then only when these two conditions are met: 1) the reader must want to know the information, and 2) the story cannot go on without this information. In a military story, the briefing/planning scene is technically exposition (telling), but when both conditions are met it is acceptable.

Watch also for two categories of telling you might not normally think of. I call them *sneaky telling* and *telling in quotation marks*.

Sneaky telling is when you slide in little bits of telling but you don't give a full information dump. So Veronica doesn't get out of her VW bug, she gets out of her lime green VW bug that she bought in Cleveland after her big breakup with Lawrence. Do you see where it ceases being showing and steps into the land of telling? (Hint: It's right at the spot where the camera can no longer see what's being talked about.) And when the phone rings, it's not Jim who stands up to answer it, it's Jim the former Navy SEAL who gets up to answer it.

If you're smuggling in little bits of telling—things the camera can't see and the reader hasn't gleaned from what the camera *can* see—you're cheating. You're telling. Avoid sneaky telling.

Also avoid telling in quotation marks. That looks like this:

> "My, Jim, isn't it nice that we're standing here before the Jedediah Smith Redwoods State Park?"
>
> "Oh, yes, Barbara. And, as you know, this forest, established in 1929, is a 10,000-acre predominately old-growth coastal redwoods

park that is bisected by the last major free flowing river in California, the Smith River."

"Why, yes. And who would've thought that almost all of the park land is a watershed for the Smith River and Mill Creek, a major tributary?"

"I know!"

Telling in quotation marks is pure exposition, just like outright telling, but the author thinks he has converted it from telling to showing by having a character say it. Not so, kemo sabe.

Remember, telling is stopping the story to explain something the reader doesn't care about. Just putting quotation marks around an information dump doesn't magically make it not an information dump. Don't stop the story to explain something—especially in the first fifty pages.

A third category of telling is flashbacks. I'm not saying that all flashbacks are telling or that you should never include them. But if your whole purpose for doing a flashback is to reveal backstory, it's de facto telling. You're still stopping the story (the main, present-day story) to explain something, and it's probably something the reader doesn't care about. Don't indulge your desire to explain everything. Just because the camera can see an acted-out flashback doesn't mean you still haven't stopped the story to dump information on your reader. Avoid flashbacks if you can.

CONVERTING TELLING TO SHOWING

In your first fifty pages there will certainly be things the reader needs to know. I'm not against conveying information in fiction. You have to do that. What I'm against is doing so in an obtrusive, boring way that stops the story. But now I've just kicked out from under you the easiest way to serve up all that information. So if you can't just sit down and type out the history and reasons and motivations behind everything that's about to happen, how can you convey this stuff to the reader?

"That, Detective, is the right question."

First, decide what the reader actually does need to know right now. You as the novelist will know one hundred times more about your characters and story world than the reader will ever need to know. I understand it hurts to not share all the awesome things you've thought of, but frankly, the reader doesn't care about most of it.

Ever talk with someone who has information you need but won't get to the point? "Oh, yes, I know the combination to your mother's safe. You know, we got that safe on sale at Woolworth's. They were going out of business, which was sad because as a kid I'd loved going to Woolworth's. They had this display of candy machines right at the front, and I'd always beg my mother to ..."

Maddening, no? Don't you just want to throttle the person and say, "I'm sure that's a great story, but would you please just give me the combination?"

That's what you do to your reader when you front-load your novel with telling. He's sure it's probably all very interesting information, but would you please just get on with the story?

If readers have little patience with a novel that has telling in its first fifty pages, how do you think editors and agents—who see this kind of thing all day long—feel about it? It's a good way for your book to catch the next train to Rejectionville.

The rule is to provide the reader with the bare minimum she needs to comprehend what's going on in the current scene. If the ground is shaking and the reader needs to know that it's not an earthquake, exactly, but a nearby volcano about to erupt, that information has to be conveyed somehow. Do we care yet that seven hundred years ago this very same volcano erupted and changed the course of the river at the bottom of the hill? Not so much. Later, maybe, but not now when the trees are falling over and the earth just swallowed the hero's ex-girlfriend's yappy dog. Just give us the least we need to know to understand what's happening.

Now that you've decided what must be conveyed to the reader, how should you convey it?

Probably 95 percent of the need-to-know information you're going to convey to the reader will be done through *action*, *dialogue*, and *scene*. Things the camera can see (and the microphone can "hear" and the smell-o-meter can smell, and so on).

How could you convey through action that the shaking of the earth is being caused by a volcano?

Think about it. Wrack that brain of yours. What action could you point the camera at that would say, "It's not an earthquake; it's a volcano"?

Do you feel that kind of mild squeezing pain? That's your brain muscle working the "showing, not telling" center of the frontal lobe. (Didn't know you had a portion of the brain dedicated to creating good fiction? Now you know!)

How about having everyone run out of a house shouting "Earthquake!" At which point someone looks off-camera, points up the hill, and shouts. Everyone turns to look, and you cut to a shot of a nearby volcano sending up small clouds of fume.

Was the information conveyed? Yes. Could the camera see it? Yes. Mission accomplished.

What about conveying the same information through dialogue? Go on, think it through. Push that muscle. Feel the burn.

How about having someone from the village call the local police to report the earthquake? In the police station that gets the call, there happens to be a volcanologist student home for spring break.

Torrance put his cigarette in the tray and grabbed the phone. "Ungar Province Police and Jail, what is your emergency?"

"Hurry!" a man said over the phone. He sounded frantic, and there was some kind of static on the line. "You must come! There is an earthquake!"

"Earthquake? Are you sure? Where are you?"

Torrance saw his nephew all but jump out of his chair when he said *earthquake*. The kid studied this stuff, didn't he? Maybe he could be useful after all.

"We are in the village of Santa Poco," the caller said. "Please, hurry!"

Torrance stood and began strapping on his holster. "All right, we will send a car. It will be—"

"Wait!" his nephew said, reaching for the phone. "Let me talk to him."

Torrance handed over the phone and went looking for his flashlight.

"Señor," he heard his nephew say into the phone, "Santa Poco—your village, how near are you to Mount Carabojo?"

Torrance couldn't hear the answer, but he knew the village was right at the base of ... No.

His nephew covered the phone with his hand and looked intensely at Torrance. "This is no earthquake, Uncle. You are about to have a volcano eruption."

Now, which is more interesting, that dialogue exchange or this:

"The people in the village thought it was an earthquake but it was really a volcano"?

Yes, it takes a lot longer to show than it does to tell, and showing conveys less detailed information than telling is capable of, but it's so much more interesting. What you lose in detail, you more than make up in reader engagement.

Read that again: What you lose in detail (when you show instead of tell), you more than make up in reader engagement. Do you want a fully informed reader or an engaged reader?

Delivering information through dialogue is much better than outright telling. But remember to avoid telling in quotation marks. It has to come across as a realistic scene that is actually interesting to watch.

Which has more impact, me saying, "He was a jerk," or you watching the guy come home, smack his toddler in the forehead, kick the cat, and yell, 'Woman, where's my dinner'?" When you *tell,* the information has no impact on the reader. She may not even remember it. But when you *show,* oh baby, now we're on.

The third way to convey information is through *scene.* Obviously the two ways mentioned already (action and dialogue) take place in scenes, but here I mean something bigger.

If you need to convey something larger, like the fact that Roy was in combat during his deployment to Afghanistan and is still suffering from the ordeal, you may want to craft an entire scene around the revelation of this information. You could simply write, "Roy saw action during his deployment to Afghanistan and is still suffering from the ordeal," but I hope you know now that, since the camera can't see it, it's telling and a very boring way to deliver information. You're making a movie (sort of), so you want to do it in front of the camera.

True, you could communicate this data through action and/or dialogue. You could have someone pick up his Purple Heart medal and say, "Dude, I totally forgot you got wounded in Afghanistan. Are you all healed up from that now?" That works for some things. But if this is centerpiece information, and especially if you need to convey more detail, you want to make it into a full-blown scene. A set piece.

How could you create a fifteen-page scene that organically brings about the divulgence and disclosure of the details of Roy's trauma in Afghanistan (without resorting to a flashback)?

Work that frontal lobe, my friend. Push!

I'm going to leave this one to do as an exercise, if you wish.

When you think about your own novel—and especially the major information that needs to be conveyed in the first fifty pages—come up with scenes to reveal it naturally. And because you're always looking for your scenes to do double and triple duty, you can use the opportunity to reveal character, develop relationships, and introduce plot elements.

THE DUMB PUPPET TRICK

I said earlier that 95 percent of your information should be conveyed through action, dialogue, and scene. Another, say, 3 percent can be conveyed through something like a briefing scene mentioned above. The last 2 percent we'll use a trick for.

Years ago I wrote puppet scripts for kids. It was sometimes useful to bring on what I called the dumb puppet. If Klibber and Clobber were talking about collecting donations for needy kids, especially if they both already knew what they were doing, I didn't want the conversation to go like this:

> Klibber: Hey, Clobber, isn't it great that we've collected all these donations?
>
> Clobber: It sure is, Klibber. Those needy kids are going to love it.

Ick, right? Telling in quotation marks. It's got to go. But what to do about it?

I'd bring on Goober, of course! The dumb puppet. (Like most "dumb" characters, he had more common sense than anyone else in the show, but I digress.) So now it went something like this:

Goober: Hey, Clobber. Hey, Klibber. What's going on?

Klibber: Oh, hi, Goober. We're just collecting.

Goober: Collecting what? Dust? Har-har-har.

Clobber: Um, no. We're taking up a collection for needy kids.

Goober: Knee-deep kids? Can't they get out? Are they in the swamp?

Klibber: Not knee-deep, Goober—Needy! Needy!

Goober: Nee-deep, nee-deep. You sound like a frog, Klibber! Nee-deep. Nee—

Clobber: Goober! We're taking up a collection of food and clothes to give to kids who don't have enough.

Goober: [*gasps*] Really? That's great! Why didn't you say so in the first place?

Okay, maybe it's not going to win a kiddie Oscar, but you can see what happened, I think. Two characters who already knew what was going on were standing there. I needed to get the information to the audience of what they were doing, but I didn't want them to go into an "As you know ..." kind of exchange. So I brought on the dumb puppet, and suddenly all of that information came flowing out—in an organic and entertaining way (that also revealed character and relationship).

The power of the dumb puppet.

In your fiction, you can tap into this power, too. When you need to convey some piece of information, and for whatever reason you're stuck about how to do it, consider bringing on a dumb puppet.

Your dumb puppet character doesn't have to be dumb, by the way. He simply has to be someone who doesn't know what's going on and has a reason to ask. Children are great at this because they don't mind asking the obvious questions. Tourists, reporters, and socially awkward brothers are also good candidates. The character of Dr. Melissa Reeves in *Twister* is a movie-length dumb puppet. She's very intelligent, but she doesn't know the world of tornado science … so she asks. And that helps us. Your dumb puppet can be anyone who might logically ask the question that will cause the information to be surfaced and thereby conveyed to the reader.

Sometimes you just can't bring on a dumb puppet. Two characters are stuck in a gondola high above the Swiss Alps, so no new person is going to happen onstage and start asking questions. Happily, there's a variant of the dumb puppet trick that can help you in this situation. It's the argument.

People rarely talk about things they already know. Unless they're fighting.

"I thought you were going to pack some water for this trip."

"Why would *I* pack water when you're carrying the pack? I asked to carry it and you said no. Trying to prove to Suzanne that you're not a loser, weren't you, Mr. Pack-Man? Well, guess what, Casanova—look at us. We're stuck in this gondola with no water and no Suzanne, and you look like more of a loser than ever!"

"Oh, yeah? Well, if you hadn't told Suzanne I was an invalid, I wouldn't need to prove anything!"

"You *are* an invalid. Look at you! Can't even stand up on a snowboard!"

And so it could go. Look at all the information that came out: Suzanne, snowboarding accidents, vying for a girl's affection—not to mention the relationship between these two characters. All because of a little argument.

If you need to get key information across to your reader, especially in the first fifty pages, start picking fights ... and out it will come.

Showing is harder than telling. Showing takes more words and more brain power. It is the path of discipline and excellence. Telling is, like the dark side of the Force, quicker, easier, and more seductive. It's lazy writing.

When in a movie can you make the screen go black while a narrator explains something? I hope you'd answer, "Never." That's how often you should stop your novel to explain something. Convey it all in ways the camera can see. But if you feel you absolutely must stop the story to explain something, please, for the sake of your novel's chances at publication, don't do it in the first fifty pages.

POINT OF VIEW

Point of view (POV) refers to whose eyes we're seeing a scene through. Clumsy POV is a surefire indicator to an agent or acquisitions editor that the author doesn't have the skill set required of a published writer.

A writer either knows how to use POV correctly or she doesn't. So POV errors usually show up in the first pages, giving an easy "no" to that project. So it is imperative that you get POV mastered, and quickly.

Can you detect whose head we are in this passage from Brad Meltzer's *The Inner Circle*?

> "Beecher, you're so ... you're handsome!"

My heart reinflates, nearly bursting a hole in my chest. Did she just—?

"You are, Beecher! You turned out great!"

My line. That's my line, I tell myself, already searching for a new one. *Pick something good. Something kind. And genuine. This is your chance. Give her something so perfect, she'll dream about it.*

"So ... er ... Clemmi," I finally say, rolling back and forth from my big toes to my heels as I notice her nose piercing, a sparkling silver stud that winks right at me. "Wanna go see the Declaration of Independence?"

Kill me now.

We're clearly in Beecher's head here. We are privy to his thoughts, his emotions, and the things he notices.

In every scene you should have one character through whose eyes we are allowed to see what's happening (and through whose brain we are interpreting it all). Here's the rule: one head per scene. Pick a head.

A couple of things to notice about Meltzer's passage. First, it's in present tense, which is pretty unusual and should probably be avoided for your first couple of novels. Dialogue is always in present tense, of course, but narrative should be rendered in the more traditional past tense: he *said*, not *says*.

Second, Meltzer uses first-person POV here. First-person POV is the "I" and "me" form of giving the viewpoint character's thoughts, as in "My heart reinflates."

Probably the most common POV in modern fiction is third person, which is the "he said/she said" form. In the above passage, it would be "His heart reinflates."

Both first-person and third-person POV are good choices for your novel. Just be sure to stay inside one head per scene.

Novels from a couple of generations ago—and some very popular novels today—hop around from head to head within a scene. These novelists would've rendered Meltzer's scene something like this:

> "Beecher, you're so ... you're handsome!" She can't believe how he's blossomed.
>
> His heart reinflates, nearly bursting a hole in his chest. Did she just—?
>
> Clemmi looked at his strong jaw and late-afternoon stubble and wondered what it would be like to kiss him. "You are, Beecher! You turned out great!"
>
> *My line. That's my line*, he tells himself, already searching for a new one. *Pick something good. Something kind. And genuine. This is your chance. Give her something so perfect, she'll dream about it.*
>
> "So ... er ... Clemmi," he finally says, rolling back and forth from his big toes to his heels as he notices her nose piercing, a sparkling silver stud that winks right at him. "Wanna go see the Declaration of Independence?"
>
> *Kill me now.*

Did you feel yourself head-hopping? First you were in Clemmi's head, and then you were in Beecher's. Then back to Clemmi, then back to Beecher, like a ping-pong ball.

This is called omniscient POV (though some call it omniscient third person ... same difference). It means you get everyone's thoughts. You're inside everyone's head.

It's not technically wrong, so please don't write me to say, "Well, what about this author? He writes like this and his books are bestsellers." I'm not saying it's wrong. I'm saying it's not ideal. I'll go so far as to say that head-hopping, like telling, is lazy writing.

Our filmmaking metaphor helps us again. Let's say you're making *Cloverfield*. The audience will see only what the character holding the camera sees. In that case, we may get to hear that character's thoughts (like maybe he's mumbling so just the camera's microphone could hear it but no one else could), but we don't get anyone else's thoughts. All we get of other characters is what they say, what they do, and what it *looks like* they're thinking. That's good POV.

Omniscient POV and telling are linked in that they both allow the author to express her urge to explain everything. The same author who wants to tell you everyone's life history also wants to tell you what everyone is thinking and why. It's this explain-itis that besets some writers. Jumping from head to head allows her to make everything manifest and leave nothing ambiguous.

Resist, I say!

The other failing of omniscient POV is that you can't withhold information from the reader. You can't keep her in the dark. So if Jeremy the gardener is really Jeremy the serial killer, one hop into ol' J's head, and we know all about his plans to kill the next eight people. So much for wondering whodunit.

Even if head-hopping is not technically wrong, it has for the most part fallen out of favor in modern fiction—largely because of the influence of cinema. The acquisitions editor or agent looking at your first fifty pages will likely know that omniscient POV is a technically allowable choice, but he will also know that it's not usually done and that it often goes hand-in-hand with telling and a generally inexpert fiction technique.

Think of your reader as sitting in a submarine with no windows. The sub is motoring along just under the surface, and the periscope is up. The world outside the sub is the world of your story. How will the reader experience your story? Why, through the periscope, of course.

The periscope is your viewpoint character.

Can the reader see what's happening in Central Park right now? No, because the viewpoint character can see only open sea and isn't within visual range of Central Park. If the viewpoint character can't see it, hear it, or know it, *neither can the reader.* Can the reader know what's happening in the area right around the sub? Of course—because the viewpoint character knows what's happening right around the sub.

Here's a tricky one: Can the reader know that the sun is glinting off the lens of the periscope? No, because the periscope can't see what the periscope itself looks like. That would require a set of eyes—er, lenses—other than the periscope's. If you told us about the glint, you'd be committing a POV error, because it's something the viewpoint character can't see, hear, or know.

So this, "Jennifer reached out her willowy arms, her eyes glistening in the moonlight, and wondered if Maurice could still love her," is a POV error. Unless she's sitting around thinking, "My, I have willowy arms," and unless she happens by a mirror that shows her eyes glistening in the moonlight, this is information coming to us from other than her own mind, which makes it a mistake.

Point of view is one of those things you need to master right away. It will show up as correct or incorrect on page 1, and throughout your first fifty pages and beyond. So if you hope to keep this publishing industry professional reading for the whole duration of your book, you must figure out POV.

❧• CHARACTER CREATION •❧

As I mentioned, I have written an entire book on how to create differentiated and realistic characters for fiction. If you know you are strong with plot but weak with character creation, I encourage you to snag a copy of *Plot Versus Character* from Writer's Digest Books.

(Conversely, if you're strong with characters but don't know what to have them do, I also recommend *Plot Versus Character*.)

But I won't leave you completely hanging here.

Weak, undifferentiated characters are sometimes harder to detect than other errors in the first fifty pages of a novel, but agents and acquisitions editors are looking for this as they evaluate fiction proposals.

The way you can tell if characters are weak is by reading, well, about fifty pages of a novel. If by then you can't tell the characters apart aside for cosmetic things like gender, age, role, office, species, attitude, or goofy accent, there's a problem. If you could switch the names around in a dialogue scene and nothing seems out of the ordinary, the characters are weak. If you've got Smythe the proper Brit with the stiff upper lip and Han the Chinese scientist and Bubbles the airhead blonde—a book peopled with stereotypes, in other words—this one will not be published. If the only difference between David and Hooper is that David's always mad and Hooper always talks dirty, the book is doomed.

Your characters must not only look different and talk and dress different, they must *seem* different from one another. Plot-first novelists can sometimes string a reader along with interesting action, but within the first fifty pages, the reader will gain the ability to see through the flash to the characters themselves. If what she sees is a group of clones who, except for external details, feel exactly like one another (or are shallow stereotypes), she's not going to want to read on.

Character-first novelists, on the other hand, create brilliant characters but tend to despair of finding anything interesting for these fascinating people to do. Their first fifty pages will usually be characterized by a lack of an engaging hook and a complete absence of suspense, stakes, or reader interest. If this is you, get a book that will help you find your story and give it proper structure.

If you know you're a plot-first novelist, don't just hope to brush by that and maybe get lucky enough to encounter an agent or acquisitions editor who won't care that your characters are undifferentiated. You have to do the hard work of learning how to create realistic, three-dimensional characters. Find a good book on the subject, and do it.

Be careful, though. When you create believable, internally consistent characters, they may not be willing to do the plot things you want them to do. I don't mean this in some mystical sense: that they'll get up and refuse to do your bidding. I mean that you'll suddenly realize that Ebenezer would never stop to help the girl in the car, which messes up your whole plot!

But do the character work anyway. Rewrite the book to let them behave as they really would. Your book with its weak characters but perfectly operating plot was probably not going to get published anyway. So why not do the work of strengthening the characters and letting them behave realistically? Because *that* will give your book a much better chance of getting published.

❧· THE EMBERS OF HOPE ·❧

So, like Strider leading the broken Fellowship of the Ring out of the long dark of Moria, you emerge from your time in the mysterious mind of an acquisitions editor.

Now you understand that she actually wants to love your book, which ought to encourage you. Publishers need to find new books to publish. They die without them. And they need to find new authors, too. For one thing, they can pay new authors less than established best-selling authors. [*grin*] But many of these editors, and their agent counterparts, dearly love discovering new voices. They want your proposal to be the one that soars to the top of their list. They want to take your proposal to PubCo and champion it before the suits. They want to be the one who discovered [insert your name here].

But the acquisitions editor is jaded. She's read thousands of proposals and found less than 1 percent that were worth investigating further, and most of those ended up not panning out. So she does want to love your first fifty pages, but she suspects she will not. Probability dictates that yours will be one of the 99 percent that won't be what she's looking for.

When she turns to your pages, she's riding that feeling of hoping-against-hope pessimism—or mostly doubtful optimism. And it's your job to beat the statistics. It's your opportunity to fan the dying ember of hope and bring it to flame.

You do that by creating an incredible first fifty pages. And you do *that* by doing several things right (which we now turn our attention to) and by avoiding these many missteps I've been talking about.

In the end, the answer isn't to eliminate the editors, but to eliminate the errors.

And now we shift from the slightly anxiety-producing discussion of what to be sure to avoid to the inspiring I-can-do-this exploration of how to create the most incredible first fifty pages that the editor, agent, or reader has seen in a very long time.

PART 2

WHAT YOUR
FIRST 50 PAGES
MUST ACCOMPLISH

We have it in our power to begin the world over again.—**THOMAS PAINE**

IN THE FINAL ANALYSIS, THERE ARE ONLY TWO THINGS you must do with your first fifty pages, only two large-scale tasks that must be accomplished:

You must engage your reader. That is Job One.

And you must set up the story so the rest of it will work correctly.

For the remainder of this book we'll be exploring the many components of each of these two tasks, but as we embark I think it's useful to get the strategic picture in your mind.

You can write the most perfectly structured story in the world, but if you don't capture your reader's interest, your novel will fail. And you can engage your reader expertly, but if you don't build the proper foundation for the rest of the novel, that engagement will eventually peter out, and he'll put your book down in frustration.

Thus far in *The First 50 Pages* we've concentrated on how agents and acquisitions editors think. That was helpful to you, I hope, in understanding what goes on in publishing decisions. I spent a good amount of time talking about what things to avoid if you want to keep that agent or editor reading, in the hope that she will want to try to get your novel published.

In that section we spoke about the reader—as in the lay reader, the person who buys your book at the bookstore—but only secondarily. For the rest of this book we'll be looking at this person as your primary audience. The things that work for the lay reader will also work for the agent or editor, but when it comes to writing fiction, it's most natural to speak in terms of writer and reader.

❧ A GLIMPSE INTO THE FUTURE ❧

How do you engage your reader? And how can you be sure you've set your novel up so the rest of it will work correctly? Those are the topics for the rest of the book, so let me introduce the subjects here.

In short, you engage your reader by making him care. You create in him a connection with the protagonist. You bring him to the point that he is pulling for your hero—or is at least curious to see what will happen to him. The hero in *Planet of the Apes* is not exactly cuddly, but we're interested enough in his situation to see how his tale will play out.

The next question, of course, is how do you make the reader care? How do you establish that connection between reader and hero? You show how the protagonist is likable. You show her striving for something but failing. You show her suffering in some way that makes the reader feel compassion for her.

Those answers may be maddening to you, because each one carries with it the following question, "Well, how do I do *that?*" No worries. We'll cover it all. This is just the introduction, right? It makes you want to read more. (One of the sub-tasks of a beginning is to make the reader want to keep reading to find out the answers, after all.)

How do you craft your first fifty pages so they start the novel out right and give the rest a strong foundation to build upon? You start the story with action of some sort. You establish the stakes and the conflict. You introduce the protagonist and let us know what his hopes are, which thereby gives us the story question. You introduce your major characters. You establish the "before" context of the story to help the reader understand how what follows is a deviation from what the protagonist had been expecting.

You introduce the antagonist and show what that person is trying to do. You reveal what the main action or challenge of the story is going to be. You show the reader the novel's genre, era, setting, backdrop, and mood. You reveal the ticking time bomb and you start it ticking. You set up the protagonist's flaw or "knot" and show us how it is affecting him at the outset. You show what is likable and heroic about your hero. You bring on the main story's first intrusion into the protagonist's world, and you send your hero off on the detour that leads to his moment of truth.

There's a Greek proverb that says, "The beginning is the half of every action." That's true with writing a great novel. If you get the first fifty pages right, you have a tenfold chance of getting the rest right. If you flub the beginning, you multiply the chances of the rest of the book failing as well.

How do you do all the things I've just breezed past? Glad you asked. Let's look at them one by one.

CHAPTER 4

ENGAGE YOUR READER

*There are two kinds of people, those who finish what they start ...
and so on.* **–ROBERT BYRNE**

WHY DO YOU CARE ABOUT LUKE SKYWALKER? WHAT connects you with Sophie (in *Sophie's Choice*)? What is it about Forrest Gump that makes you pull for him? And why, when she's such a brat, do you cheer for Scarlett O'Hara?

If you're like most folks, at several points in your life movies and novels have grabbed you on an emotional level. Sometimes it's because the story brings back highly charged memories for you or triggers the release of feelings you've got pent up because of something going on in your life. The magic of story is that it allows us to vicariously experience the emotion of the tale and feel it so deeply that it helps us to navigate our own issues.

The Greeks even had a word for it: *catharsis*. Greek theater established (or, perhaps, *recognized*) just about all of the elements of great storytelling, and we novelists stand on their shoulders today. One of these elements was the depiction onstage of a character having an extreme emotional reaction—sorrow, anger, pity, or even joy—with the intent of causing that same reaction in the audience. They understood that something we see a character going through in a made-up story can help us go through it, too, and thus achieve an emotional purging.

That's why it feels strangely positive to have "a good cry." And why we feel optimistic after laughing so hard we shed tears. There are physiological things going on in the brain chemistry, of course. But the thing to notice is that viewers of a play or movie—or readers of a novel—are willing and able to make a strong emotional connection with a character in a story.

One of the main ways to engage your reader is to make him bond with your main character. Cement his emotional connection with the hero. There are other ways to gain reader engagement, and we'll talk about those as well, but this will be your primary method. And even if it's not, why not also add reader-hero engagement to any story?

Why do we connect with Luke Skywalker? Maybe because he's an orphan, an idealist, and a dreamer longing for adventure in a fight against overwhelming evil. Oh, yes, we can sink our teeth into a story about a guy like that.

What is it about Sophie that grabs us? We identify with her because she hurts so deeply and has suffered so much and yet is still capable of love. Her suffering gives us the courage to endure our own suffering. We know what it is to feel pain, so we have a kinship with her.

Forrest Gump is simple but exceedingly loving. He's an innocent, and we want him to be protected, so we connect with him in a protective way. But he's also a doggedly loyal friend and lover. Maybe we're like him—or maybe we wish we had a Forrest in our life, someone whose love for us never faltered no matter how we'd failed.

And what about Scarlett O'Hara or George "Bright Eyes" Taylor (Charlton Heston's character in *Planet of the Apes*)? What is it about these two unlikable people that makes us unable to stop watching them? And even pull for them? They're resourceful, for one thing. They're clever and intelligent and always seem to find a way to land on their feet. They are strong personalities whose "will to power" makes us watch with fascination as they work and connive to try to master the unfortunate situations in which they find themselves. We also see hints of their compassion, and that's a key. They're crusty on the outside but have a soft middle.

If you want to engage your reader (and you do), you must cause her to emotionally connect with your protagonist.

❦ THE UNLIKABLE PROTAGONIST ❦

Have you ever read a novel or watched a movie in which the protagonist was utterly distasteful? I'm not talking just a cranky old man or a spoiled child or your run-of-the-mill anti-hero, but someone just awful?

The movie *Igor* was so hard to watch because, among other reasons, the main character was evil. He was bent on taking a kindhearted character and making her mean. It just wasn't someone you could cheer for. I disliked one of the newer Charlie Brown specials because nobody was likable. Everyone was a little animated jerk, which was certainly not what Charles Schulz had imagined. Roald Dahl was removed from the 1970s big screen adaptation of his *Charlie and the Chocolate Factory* because his original script made all the characters unlikable.

My question was whether you'd ever read a novel or watched a movie in which you disliked the main character. The answer is "Probably not." There are some out there, as we've seen, but not many—and you've probably not watched or read them all the way through.

When we come to read a novel, we don't want to invest however many hours reading however many pages if we're going to be stuck looking over the shoulder of an unlikable person.

Keep that in mind as you plan the protagonist of your novel. It's good to have a character with a flaw if you're going to show him overcoming it through the course of the story. But even then you can't have him start so low that he's despicable.

That's not to say you can't have dirty rotten scoundrels in your story, as the film by the same name testifies. The *Ocean's Eleven* series of movies is all about crooks, as is *The Italian Job*. *The Bourne Identity* is about an assassin. *Sneakers* is about hackers. And it wasn't *Despicable Me* and *Megamind* that invented bad guys with a good side. Look at Darth Vader and Gollum (from *The Lord of the Rings*) and Don Corleone (from *The Godfather*). All three are villains, yet they have something redeeming in them trying to get out.

But it's the good that makes us tolerate them and even come to like them or pull for them. That's the key element. And you'll note that those characters were not the protagonists of their stories.

So, in your book, is your hero a nice person? It's okay—virtually required, actually—for her to have some flaw that the story is going to pound out of her. But she has to be somewhat likable at the outset, or you'll lose your reader before things even get going.

❧· HOW TO MAKE YOUR PROTAGONIST LIKABLE ·❧

There are as many specific methods for building a reader's connection with a character as there are characters. But they fall into five general categories.

To cause your reader to engage with your hero, make your protagonist heroic, principled, sympathetic, winsome, or smart.

THE HEROIC PROTAGONIST

By heroic, I don't necessarily mean that the protagonist be granted superhero powers or that he has to be an über warrior on the battlefield. By *heroic,* I mean willing to sacrifice and risk for the benefit of others.

Ellen Ripley (Sigourney Weaver's character in the *Alien* movies) is not a very nice person. But she risks her life to save others—including her cat (in the first film) and a little girl (in the second). She is willing to suffer potential harm and death, not to mention terror, in order to rescue someone who is in danger. *That's* a hero we can cheer for.

Samwise Gamgee (from *The Lord of the Rings*) is by nature a fairly timid fellow, preferring to work in his garden rather than take on Ringwraiths and other terrors. But when his beloved Frodo is in danger, little Sam goes toe-to-toe with a giant spider creature, dispatches sundry villains, and would march directly into the Cracks of Doom if it would mean sparing his friend. Who couldn't connect with a character like that?

M'Lynn Eatenton (Sally Field's character in *Steel Magnolias*) can be a real overbearing pest, so driven she has become to protect her adult daughter, Shelby. But when Shelby needs a kidney, M'Lynn doesn't hesitate. A woman who would give her kidney for her daughter? Perhaps it's something most mothers would do, but it remains a deeply heroic act, and this endears M'Lynn to us.

As I was writing this, Japan was recovering from a massive earthquake and tsunami that left thousands dead and missing. The nuclear plants damaged in the tragedy were in danger of melting down. Most everyone had been evacuated. But for a few days, fifty workers remained behind to try to stave off a complete disaster. These men and women—the Fukushima 50—may well have sacrificed or at least shortened their lives in order to attempt to save their countrymen. That's heroic, and if someone wanted to write a novel about those workers, that book would have characters the reader would definitely find engaging.

What about your novel? Do you find your hero heroic? If so, somewhere in the first fifty pages you need to give us a glimpse of that. You don't have to show her running into a burning building to save a child, but you might show her standing up for someone who is getting picked on at work. Your reader wants to engage with your main character, and a great way to achieve that is to make your hero selfless and willing to suffer loss for the sake of another. Why not work that into your book?

THE PRINCIPLED HERO

Sturm Brightblade is a character in the *Dragonlance* fantasy novels by Tracy Hickman and Margaret Weis. Sturm is a Knight of Solamnia, an order of warriors who live by a code of honor. While other characters might engage in thievery or prostitution, Sturm will not. While others might set an ambush to trick an enemy force, Sturm cannot. He would prefer marching out and challenging the enemy to a fair fight—even if it was a hopeless situation—to resorting to trickery.

Sturm's scruples were often maddening to his companions. They would have to "handle" him and keep him away from scenarios in which his code would force him to behave in a certain way, which would put them all in danger. He would be the object of scorn, and would seem to have a much less good time, in certain other encounters.

But while people might object to Sturm's internal code of conduct, it was impossible not to like the man. He held to a system of behavior even when no one else was there to check up on him. He was a man of character. We might not agree with his ethics, but we could not say he had none. A person who stands by a personal code, even in the face of ridicule, is someone with whom we will connect.

There is something heroic (there's that word again) and altogether *right* about restricting oneself to a set of idealistic parameters. We will all draw those lines in different places, but even villains have things they simply won't do. Except for the sociopaths among us, we all have a conscience. It's like this invisible voice informing us when we're coming close to a personal line in the sand. Even if we choose to cross that line, it's significant that the line was there. And when we see someone make a choice—to do something or withhold from doing something—because of this silent advisor, we understand. We may not agree, but we do understand.

So it is with fiction. Azeem (Morgan Freeman's character in *Robin Hood: Prince of Thieves*) must stop and pray toward Mecca several times a day, and when everyone else is celebrating with beer and mead, he says, "Alas, Allah forbids it." The other characters may be sad that he doesn't join them in reveling, but you almost get the sense that Azeem actually rises in their estimation because of his commitment to character and his beliefs.

The TV series *24* seemed to be all about placing its principled characters into morally ambiguous situations. The best of them seemed always to be drowning in a morass of gray area. It was fascinating to watch people try to do the right thing when the right thing was anything but clear. Even if the character made a decision that resulted in things going badly, we applauded that person who tried to find the higher path.

To make your reader connect with your hero, give your hero an internal code. Make her a person of character. Show her striving to do right in the face of the compromise around her, even when no one else is there to judge, and we will become deeply engaged.

THE SYMPATHETIC HERO

"I got a rock."

Poor Charlie Brown. Somehow the universe knows he's the guy to pick on. He's the one to get a rock instead of candy in his Halloween bag. He's the one whose kites always get eaten by the kite-eating tree. He's the one who always gets blasted off the pitcher's mound by every batter he faces.

And yet ol' Chuck still loves his dog and still believes in the spirit of Christmas and still hopes that this time he'll finally kick that football.

Charlie Brown is a sympathetic character. Hard things happen to him, but he endures. And the worse it seems for him, the more we pull for him.

That's the power of reader engagement.

Earlier, I mentioned Sophie in *Sophie's Choice*. She hurts, and we hurt right along with her. We connect with her.

Have you ever noticed how many Disney characters are orphans? From Mowgli to Cinderella to Tarzan to Ariel, they're usually missing their mother, if not both parents. Just by nature of that missing maternal figure, the character becomes sympathetic. We feel the hole in the character's heart, and we yearn for that person to find love and belonging to help fill that hole.

You can make your hero sympathetic in other ways besides playing the orphan card. Show her trying at something and failing yet again. She doesn't make the basketball team—again. The cast list is posted, but someone else got the part she wanted. The boy she'd been sweet on shows up with some bimbo on his arm. The letter arrives from the scholarship committee, but she has not gotten the scholarship. She's got her new outfit on, and a bus splashes her with mud.

Now, you don't want to make your hero too much of a sad sack or readers will go from compassion to disgust. It's one thing to be treated like a loser; it's something else to *be* a loser.

Think about your novel. How could you show your hero as sympathetic? Is she lonely? Is he cut off from some relationship or achievement he craves? Has she spent long hours preparing something, but someone still minimizes her work? Does he have a critical father?

You want to make us feel sorry for your hero. Not in the sense of disdain, but in the sense that we want to pull for her to succeed.

THE WINSOME HERO

Why do we love Forrest Gump? Why do we love Gilligan? What about Chauncey Gardiner (Peter Sellers's character in *Being There*) or the Tin Man or Sheldon (in *The Big Bang Theory*) or Inspector Clouseau?

One reason we engage with these characters is that we find them endearing. They are good souls. They make us laugh. They are gentle. And there's a purity about them that reminds us of children.

Neo (Keanu Reeves's character in *The Matrix*) is caught up in something big and violent. But he makes time for children, gives of himself, and helps his landlady carry out her garbage. He's a nice guy.

Captain Jack Sparrow (Johnny Depp's character in the *Pirates of the Caribbean* movies) is a cad and a scalawag, but he is (mostly) loyal to his friends and makes us laugh. He's flamboyant and outrageous, but utterly delightful.

As Jack shows us, your characters don't have to be heroes (as in on the right side of the law) to be likable. The bumbling henchmen in *101 Dalmatians* come to mind, as do all of Gru's minions in *Despicable Me*. And in "Mother" (Dan Aykroyd's character in *Sneakers*), you'll never find a more delightful crook.

Can you make your hero winsome? Can you show how he's funny and kind and good-hearted? If you can, it will be a great way to get your reader to attach to him. Keep in mind that you'll need to at least initially reveal this winsomeness somewhere in the first fifty pages.

THE SMART HERO

The final way to make readers engage with your hero is to make your hero smart. Resourceful. Clever. Mentally agile.

Sometimes life can feel like being buried under an avalanche at a puzzle factory. Nothing seems simple. Everything is concealed and incomplete and mixed up. The world seems confusing, and we can never seem to find the edges or see around the corner or over the next hill.

Maybe that's why we like detective stories so much. Here's a world-class mind pitted against the kind of baffling mystery that perplexes us daily. We value characters who can see straight through the smoke to the thing the smoke was meant to conceal. We delight in seeing a resourceful hero trying to climb to the top of that pile of puzzles to tell us what she sees from there.

And so Sherlock Holmes and Miss Marple and Hercule Poirot and Adrian Monk and Patrick Jane (Simon Baker's character on *The Mentalist*) become our friends and heroes.

But it's not just detectives who make us engage with them because of their heroic smarts. We cheer for Elle Woods (Reese Witherspoon's character in *Legally Blonde*) as she uses her wits to seize her dreams. Scott Pilgrim proves remarkably resourceful against all manner of video game villains in *Scott Pilgrim vs. the World*. Erin Brockovich, though she is a real person and not a fictional creation, seems an unlikely person to bring down a corrupt power supply company, but she does it.

One of the most delightful reveals I've seen of a character's grand strategy comes near the end of *Down With Love*. I won't spoil it for you, but suffice it to say that Barbara Novak (Renée Zellweger's character) has spent pretty much the entire movie playing out an elaborate scheme to achieve her objective. It's staggering in its complexity, but we gain an enormous connection with her when we see what she's done.

What about in your novel? Can you make your main character smart, clever, or resourceful? Can you give him a way of staying a step ahead of the pack? Can she have a penchant for knowing what to do when others around her stand scratching their heads? Could he always be working on an invention or strategy that no one else has thought of?

We like smart characters. We want to see if they can solve the riddle posed to them. If you want your reader to engage with your hero, make her clever.

Keep in mind that you can combine these elements to make the reader certain to engage with your hero, and thus your story. It's no accident that Luke Skywalker is a hero with whom audiences have connected for generations. He's a heroic, idealistic orphan who lives by a code of conduct. He's resourceful and good-hearted, and he can even make us laugh, if only at his youthful desire to win the princess's heart.

To cause readers to engage with your story, which is Job One with your first fifty pages, you need to have them emotionally connect with your hero.

❧· OTHER WAYS TO ENGAGE YOUR READER ·❧

The best way to cause your reader to buy in to your story is to make her pull for your hero. But there are other ways to achieve this as well.

One of these is to grab the reader through *action*. Think of how any James Bond film begins. Incredible action set piece, eye-popping stunts and gadgets, speed and thrills and fights and derring-do. If you can watch 007 get thrown out of an airplane without a parachute yet still find a way to survive (*Moonraker*) and not be hooked as a viewer, you might want to seek counseling. Seriously.

If you can watch the opening sequence of *Star Trek* (the 2009 version), in which a character is captain of a starship for twelve minutes and saves eight hundred lives, and not be ready to see the story through to the end, something's wrong. The battle at the beginning of *Gladiator* is a thing of savage beauty. We want to see more of this.

Hook us with action.

Now, what if you don't want something to explode or have someone dropped out of an airplane? No problem. It's quite possible to grab your reader by means of something a little more sedate. In that case, you engage readers by *intriguing* them.

The Hunt for Red October starts with a Soviet submarine plowing through a brutally cold Russian morning. We see Sean Connery speaking his good ol' Scots-Russian brogue. There's something about his eyes. He's making a decision, setting out on an irrevocable course. What's he going to do with this sub? And since when is Sean Connery a Russian? There are enough questions here—plus a heroic Russian army chorus and a soaring hymn to the Revolution—that we can't help wondering what is about to happen. We're intrigued.

Another Russian story: *Enemy at the Gates* starts with our hero, Vassili Zaitsev, as a boy out hunting with his grandfather. We hear his thoughts as he concentrates on trying to shoot a wolf in a snowy Russian forest. The tension rises as he takes aim with his rifle but hesitates. His moment is slipping away. His grandfather is saying, "Now, Vassili. Now!" We never find out if he shoots the wolf or not. But we're intrigued. We're hooked.

Stargate begins with some village of early humans being visited by an alien spaceship that zaps one of the villagers. *Ever After* starts with the Brothers Grimm being summoned to see Jeanne Moreau, who shows them a glass slipper and says, "Once upon a time …" *Rear Window* opens with a voyeuristic survey of all the lives and apartments we can see into from our hero's rear window. None of these are big action set pieces, but they all engage your mind and make you lean forward in your chair.

You can do that with your novel.

Do you have an interesting world for your story? Can your hero do something inherently fascinating? Is the villain up to something so diabolical that readers can't help but be attracted to the story? If you think about it, I'm pretty sure you could find some way to intrigue your reader with your opening scene. Consider if that might be how you should begin.

And why not do more than one? If engaging the reader is Job One for your first fifty pages, why not be doubly or triply sure you're accomplishing it? Why not an intriguing prologue-type scene followed by an action sequence?

That's how *Enemy of the Gates* did it. Years after the young Vassili does or doesn't shoot the wolf, we join him as a young man being sent to the Battle of Stalingrad. We watch over his shoulder as Russian recruits are herded off a train onto boats, where most of them are shot out of the water by Stuka dive-bombers. The survivors are driven to the front lines, where they are goaded to charge the German machine gun entrenchments. Those Russian soldiers who turn to retreat are shot by their own officers. Talk about being engaged in the story.

And while you're at it, why not show us something likable about the hero? *Enemy at the Gates* again. We're instantly connected to Vassili because we feel his fear and see the terror of his situation. We'd already begun caring for him because of what we saw in the prologue, but now we're really on his side. After the furor of that horrific battle, we see that he has survived, and we see him use his cleverness and skill with the rifle—and even his politeness, which makes him even more likable—to perform a truly heroic feat of war.

I don't know about you, but when I began watching that movie I didn't feel especially close to any Russian snipers in World War II. It was an era of history I'd not studied, so it all seemed pretty remote. But by the end of the extended opening sequence I've just described, I was all but grafted into the skin of young Vassili Zaitsev. I almost didn't care what would happen next—I was going to see this thing through.

That is the power of an engaging opening. To take a reader from her own world and concerns and make all of that fade away until she is strapped in and raring to go wherever you're planning to take her.

❧· BUILD A CONNECTION ·❧

Engaging your reader is Job One. You can do everything else right, but if you get this wrong, the book will fail. But get this right, as in really right, and it will cover a multitude of fiction sins.

So how do you want to begin your book? How will you capture your reader? We'll talk in later chapters about the pros and cons of prologues and about how to bring your main character onstage for the first time. But right now I want you to think only about how you're going to get your reader on board for this journey.

Keep it consistent with the tone of your book. If it's a sweet romance about summer lovers, don't hook the reader with an alien invasion. You might hook him, but he'll throw the hook when he realizes you misled him. So look for a way—or ways—to intrigue or astonish your reader and build a connection to your hero.

Do that, and readers will automatically sign up for the catharsis they're looking for from your story, whether they realize they're looking for it or not.

CHAPTER 5

INTRODUCE YOUR MAIN CHARACTER

You have to walk carefully in the beginning of love; the running across fields into your lover's arms can only come later when you're sure they won't laugh if you trip. **–JONATHAN CARROLL**

IN THE PREVIOUS CHAPTER WE LOOKED AT HOW TO engage the reader. That's the most important thing you have to do in your first fifty pages. Without that, everything else is moot. But the next most important thing your opening pages have to do is create the proper foundation for the rest of the novel. Your beginning is all about setup.

We'll discuss three-act structure in a bit, but here I'll say that I consider Act 2 to be the heart of your story. It's where the real fun of the book happens. But you couldn't simply start in the middle—the reader wouldn't know what was going on. You couldn't start *Star Wars* with Luke sneaking around the Death Star. The reader would be like, "Whoa—who are these people and what's going on?" Before the fun can happen, a lot of groundwork has to be done so the rest will make sense.

And if you do it right, the groundwork will be fun, too.

The remainder of part two in *The First 50 Pages* is about doing this setup. Your book's beginning bears a surprising amount of weight and is essential to the success of the rest of the novel.

We're going to look at the components of this groundwork one at a time.

These elements could be presented in almost any order. Indeed, I spent a good deal of time playing with different organizational schemes (doing my own groundwork) before finally settling on this one.

We'll be looking at everything from revealing the story's backdrop to bringing on the villain, starting the hero's inner journey, writing your first line, and a ton of stuff in between.

The first component we'll look at is how to bring your main character onstage the first time.

❧· GREAT EXPECTATIONS ·❧

How do you get to know someone? By spending time with her, of course. It's the reason we date or go through courtship with someone: We like what we've seen so far, but we want to visit with that person more to see additional angles and learn more of the other person's layers. What we find may surprise us, for good or ill. What we thought we'd seen of this person at the outset may not be true at all.

In life, sometimes we get the wrong idea about people because of how we meet them. For instance, let's say the first time we meet a woman she's working in the church nursery and coming a little unglued because there are nine poopy babies and only six clean diapers. Then we come to find out later that this woman is the chair of the philosophy department at the local university, and she's going to be on television next week debating creation/evolution with a scholar from Scotland. It will take a little head-shaking for us to get our minds around who this person is professionally.

It works the same way in fiction. We come to know a novel's characters by spending time with them. We get first impressions of them from what we've seen on the page in the beginning. If the writer has done his job right, what we learn of them later serves to confirm and expand upon what we saw at first.

If the character we see later doesn't match what we saw in his first appearance, sometimes no amount of brain jiggling will allow us to make the shift. We'll say, "Hey, that's not who this person is. Why'd you make me think he was going to be X if he's really Y?" Readers don't always take kindly to story people acting out of character.

How you bring any of your characters onstage the first time will stay with the reader for the duration of the novel, so do it with forethought.

The single most important entrance in your book is the one in which your protagonist first takes the stage. It's amazing to me how many authors give nearly no thought to what impression they're giving readers by how they introduce their main character. In this chapter we're going to learn how to do it right.

❧· WHO IS THIS PERSON? ·❧

This is not a book on character creation for fiction. For that, I recommend my book *Plot Versus Character*. However, it does bear mentioning that you must do your character creation homework.

As I've mentioned, I'm of the opinion that all novelists are either plot-first writers or character-first writers. That is, either story ideas come to you first or characters come to mind first, begging to leap onto the page. If you're a character-first novelist, you're probably right with me when I say you've got to do your character creation work. (On the other hand, I've found that many character-firsters don't actually do their character homework, relying instead on instinct. Tsk-tsk, I say.)

If you're a plot-first novelist, you may be tempted to skip this whole section. Buy a book on character creation? Pshaw. Characters—who needs 'em? So long as I've got the hero and the girl and the sidekick and the villain, I'm golden. Oh, and José the Mexican, Gomer the grease monkey, and Smythe the uppity aristocrat. And a whole host of other stereotypes standing by ready to step onstage.

Ahem. Well, allow me to suggest that stereotypes do not good characters make. And novels with stereotypical characters—or characters who have virtually no differentiation from one another at all—are not typically published. You must figure out who your characters are.

Here's an area where the screenwriter actually gets to take a lazy path whereas the novelist has to take the way of discipline. A screenwriter can write stereotypes, but then it's up to the director, the casting director, and the actors to give depth to otherwise flat characters. The screenwriter might write a generic fop character and get away with it, because the actor—like Jeremy Piven's Versace salesman in *Rush Hour 2* or Chris Tucker's Ruby Rhod in *The Fifth Element*—will make him something so much more than just a stereotype.

But the novelist doesn't have the luxury of knowing that a gifted actor will come along and elevate the stereotype to something better fleshed out. The novelist has words on a page, and that's it. That's where the magic must happen.

So … no generic characters for you. No flat stereotypes. No characters who differ from one another only in terms of goals, moods, roles, and agendas.

I say all this because, if you're going to bring your characters on in ways that perfectly typify them and correctly establish reader expectations, which you are, you have to know who these story people are. How can you correctly portray a character's core characteristic if you don't know what that core characteristic is? (Hint: It's not "He wants to pick up chicks" or "She's mean.")

One of the vital components of your first fifty pages—nay, of your entire novel—is to depict your characters as believable individuals who are differentiated from every other character in the book. Do your character creation homework, and you'll be able to expertly craft an excellent introductory scene for each one.

❦· PROLOGUE OR CHAPTER ONE? ·❦

We discuss prologues and first pages in depth in future chapters, but I need to talk about them a bit here.

How will you begin your novel? That's the question this whole book is designed to answer, I know. But for now, just think about this: How do you envision your page 1? Do you feel your story should begin with the main character herself, or were you thinking of an opening that would be more of an action set piece that established the villain and intrigued the reader?

The reason I ask is that it will determine how you introduce your main character. If your novel is going to begin with the hero onstage, that opening scene also has to engage the reader with something interesting happening. It's good to begin building reader connection with your hero by showing her stooping to help a lost kitten, but that's probably not going to hook your reader. So now you've got to have her stoop to help the kitten while also staving off an alien invasion.

Okay, not really. But the point is that a novel that begins with the hero on the screen has to do double duty. It's got to both hook the reader and typify the protagonist. Some stories can't bear that kind of onus, and some authors feel if they did they'd be artificially thrusting the hero into action she wouldn't really be doing. In those cases, it's better to write a prologue that features other characters, and then you can bring the hero onstage in chapter one.

(More about the pros and cons of prologues in chapter nine.)

An example of a movie that begins with the hero onscreen doing something interesting would be any James Bond movie. Through the action of that opening sequence, we see a bit of who this guy is and what he's capable of. Those scenes also serve to engage the reader through action. So it is possible to do both at once. An example of a movie that begins with a prologue and then introduces the hero later would be *Atlantis: The Lost Empire* (the Disney animated film), which begins with the destruction of Atlantis and only later introduces the hero, Milo Thatch.

If you decide to begin your novel with the protagonist onstage, keep in mind that you need to craft his introduction in a way that also engages reader interest. If you're going to begin with a prologue featuring other characters, your hero's introductory scene can be a bit more leisurely, and you can concentrate on making her likable and building reader connection. The kitten may safely be swooped.

❧• CAPTURING YOUR HERO'S ESSENCE •❧

Whether you introduce your protagonist on page 1 or after a prologue, most of the tasks are the same. Your objective for your hero's introduction has a number of parts, but the first is to convey to the reader who this person is at his core. We'll certainly learn much more about this character as the story goes on, but first impressions are vital.

Who is your hero at her core? You know this now because you've done your character homework. You know what makes her tick. You know what's heroic or likable about her. You know what her issues are. You know her temperament. Now's the time to dress that up and send it out to meet the press.

Let's say your hero is a noble but depressed man who has lost his family and now wants nothing to do with anyone else … or does he? He thinks he just wants to be left alone to die, and he definitely doesn't want to be in a position to protect any other helpless people, because if he were any good at that, he wouldn't have lost his own family, right?

How would you illustrate that in a scene?

We already know we can't just say, "Jim was depressed because he lost his family tragically and now he wanted to be left alone," because that would be *telling*, which would get your book rejected by publishers. So how would you do it in a *showing* way?

Come on, work that part of your frontal lobe dedicated to good fiction. What scene could you create that would reveal this about such a character?

The process we're working on is twofold: 1) isolate the primary characteristic, and 2) depict that characteristic in a scene. And, obviously, the prerequisite for this is to identify your main character's primary characteristic. So what is it for your protagonist?

What if your hero were a woman so out of touch with her femininity that she fits in more with the guys than the girls, including the more negative aspects of traditional masculinity like a fierce independence that defies protocol and authority?

As you think about how to do this, you're necessarily factoring in elements we haven't gone over yet, like genre and setting and era. That's what I mean by how we could have talked about these components in any order. For now, don't let those other aspects of the story intrude. Think only of your hero's essence and how that might be illustrated in a scene. You can think later about how to plant that in your particular story world.

That implantation is actually easy once you have this part figured out. It's much harder to look at your story world and the mandates it puts on you and only then try to come up with a character's core and how to illustrate it. In writing fiction, it's almost always best to go from the theoretical to the practical rather than the other way around.

Take some time right now to figure out your hero's essential characteristic. Then take another few minutes to brainstorm four or five ways that characteristic could come out in a scene. You don't have to decide on one yet. Indeed, there are a number of other elements to consider before locking down that introductory scene. But this task—revealing her core in a scene—is the main part.

❧• CAN'T YOU JUST PICTURE IT? •❧

If your hero were to have his portrait made, how would he want to appear? I'm not talking about modern portraits where all you get to choose from is the black backdrop, the white backdrop, or the forest backdrop with the fencepost prop. I'm talking about old-school portraits, like those paintings done in the Renaissance, in which a person's portrait included elements that conveyed much about his passions, history, and life.

Elizabeth I of England, the Armada Portrait,
Woburn Abbey (George Gower, ca 1588)

Here's one of Queen Elizabeth I. She's arrayed in an impressive, queenly dress, and her hair's been done up for the painting. All well and good. But notice the other elements. She's got her hand on a globe. What could that mean? Something about an interest in points beyond England, certainly. Indeed, what landmass *is* that? Terra incognita, perhaps.

Her crown sits on a pedestal beside her. Why? Because she doesn't like to mess up her hair? Or because her personality is to set aside her station and just be Lizzie? I don't know, but it's intriguing. And out the windows over her shoulder … wow. Well, she's big on navies, it seems. But what is it saying? Maybe it's a before-and-after story. In the beginning, she sent out her mighty navy on a global quest under a hopeful sun. But then: storms. Wrack and ruin. Did she send them to their doom? Or is this depicting her country's conquest on the high seas? No clue.

Isn't that much more interesting than just a straight-on shot conveying only her likeness?

Now we're going to paint a portrait of your main character.

If your protagonist knew she was going to have her portrait painted in the style we've seen here, what would she have in the painting? What would she be wearing? Where would she be sitting? Would she be sitting at all? What would she have her hand on? What would be out the windows? What would be on the table next to her?

This is going back to the core characteristic, but it's expanding on it. When you know who your hero is in his essence, you can figure out ways to reveal it.

Do this for your protagonist. How would he want to be depicted in such a portrait? What elements would need to be in the image to give a snapshot of his character?

Then take the exercise a step further: Create a little movie scene that captures your hero in her element. For this, don't worry about your book's genre or setting or anything else. If she could be doing anything at all, in any time in world history (or in any otherworldly future or dimension), what would it be? This is the place to ask, "If she could drive the ultimate car, what would it be?"—even if your character will live in a time when there are no cars. Go a little crazy as you search for the best possible fit for your character.

The idea is to identify for yourself what he's really like. If this character were transported to the Twilight Zone and allowed to gravitate to the ultimate-for-him activity, what would it be?

Would he be lazing by the pool sipping a cold drink with a little umbrella in it—while dozens of rescued orphans had fun in the pool? Would she be floating in space repairing a battlecruiser in the middle of a war with the Zudokons? Would he be living high above the forest in the bole of a tree where he spends his days writing love sonnets?

What would she be doing? With whom would he be? What would she be wearing? What would he be talking or thinking about? Most important of all: Why would this be what the character chose? How is this the ultimate expression or revelation of the person's core?

When you've got this down, you're ready to bring your hero onstage for the first time.

If you're a plot-first novelist, you may be wondering why I'm "wasting" your time making you think about character stuff, but I assure you this work will pay dividends when you begin writing your novel.

Doing this work gives you a handle on who your hero really is. When she gets into a tight spot and you're not sure what she would do, come back to this little scene simulation and read it again. It will reconnect you with your character's core, and that will give you a clue on how she would respond in that situation.

Incidentally, there's much more to character creation than just this. In *Plot Versus Character*, this idealized self-portrait scene exercise is the final bit of work we do to be sure we know our character. So you'd do this plus a lot more before this. But if you're in a hurry to write or you're not yet convinced that character homework is required or if you've already done that work, this will at least help you as you begin to write your book.

❦· FOUND IN TRANSLATION ·❦

Now let's take that *Twilight Zone* scene from the rarified air of idealistic character moment and bring it to the specific climes of your story.

Earlier, we talked about a depressed character who had lost his family and just wanted to be left alone. Let's say that was

THE FIRST 50 PAGES

your protagonist, and you were writing a story about life just before an ice age. How could you reveal his essence in that context? He couldn't be living alone in a space station completely cut off from civilization, as perhaps you'd depicted him in the self-portrait exercise. He'd have to be on Earth in the days before the ice age. You might even make him something besides a human.

You might show a vast horde of prehistoric creatures migrating away from the encroaching glaciers—but one woolly mammoth is going against the tide, carving a wide path not away from the ice but toward it. He's depicted as contrary and antisocial just by his orientation in reference to everyone around him. And he's grumpy. He's going toward the place everyone else is leaving. He's depressed and he wants to be alone.

That's how we meet Manny the mammoth, the main character in *Ice Age.*

See how his core characteristic was so clearly illustrated by how we first encountered him? Very soon we will also see that, despite his curmudgeonly manner, he really does long to protect the small and weak. The filmmakers did their character homework. They thought about what their hero's core characteristics were and how they could be illustrated in the context of the story they wanted to tell. It's terrific storytelling—and you're going to do that with your book, too.

What if you had the woman who had lost touch with her feminine side? She's more comfortable in the locker room than the powder room. She's more apt to belch and spit than own a tube of lipstick. If you did your self-portrait exercise with her, you might have her being the only woman on a college football team. You might have her argue with her boss—not because the boss has done anything wrong but because the character just doesn't like having to obey anyone's rules.

Or you might have her dress in gender-neutral clothes to take part in a police sting on organized crime. You might have her go rogue and deviate from the plan because she is so unruly and so sure she's the only one who knows what's what—which might end up endangering not only the sting but the lives of her colleagues.

That's how we meet Gracie Hart, Sandra Bullock's character in *Miss Congeniality*. The writers took as their starting point the character's personality and "issues," and then had her act those out by putting her into a situation that caused them to become visible.

It's worth pointing out that both Gracie Hart and Manny the mammoth begin the story in ways that are very contrary to how they will turn out. Gracie, the extreme tomboy, will have to enter a beauty pageant and pose as the girliest of girls on the planet. And Manny, the depressed loner, will end up as the father figure in a new little family he must guide and protect.

We're still too early in this book to discuss it at length, but a good character introduction will also reveal the protagonist's starting point in his inner journey. This starting point will stand in clear contrast with where he will end up.

❧· UPON THIS, ALL DEPENDS ·❧

A great character introduction is essential to the success of your novel. It's on the short list of must-haves for any great work of fiction.

I mentioned Milo Thatch earlier (*Atlantis*). When we first see him, he's giving a scholarly presentation to the board of directors of the university. He's laying out his theory of where he believes Atlantis may be discovered. He's got maps and relics and illuminated manuscripts. He's enthusiastic and confident, despite his youth.

He's also not really talking to the board of directors. The lights come on, and we realize he's been talking to mannequins and skeletons in a mock audience. A call comes down for him—not to come make his presentation for real but to bang on the pipes of the boiler because it's not producing heat.

It's a terrific reveal that shows us both what he dreams of becoming and what he really is. We're instantly connected to him because he's got passion and intelligence, but he's underappreciated and kept from achieving his dreams. We want him to succeed—all because of a wonderful character introduction.

Think of the great introductions of Cinderella, Indiana Jones (*Raiders of the Lost Ark*), R.J. (*Over the Hedge*), Mulan, Gru (*Despicable Me*), Harry Potter, and Captain Jack Sparrow. Study these, and then decide how to craft the perfect way to bring your main character onstage the first time.

❧· INTRODUCING SECONDARY CHARACTERS ·❧

It's not only your hero who has to have a great intro. There are a handful of others whose entrance you should give thought to: your villain, your romantic interest, and any other major characters in the book.

Han Solo isn't the protagonist of *Star Wars*, but who can forget the "Sorry about the mess" intro he has in the Mos Eisley Cantina? Jon Lovitz has a knack for creating wonderful minor characters, as evidenced by his brief but brilliant roles in *The Wedding Singer, Three Amigos*, and more. Actually, the writers created those characters. That's your job.

In *Sneakers*, Liz (played by Mary McDonnell) is the romantic interest. The first time we meet her, she's in an elite conservatory school working with a gifted young pianist. Everything about her surroundings, job, dress, and demeanor bespeak class—quite a contrast to the ratty blue jeans and, well, sneakers of her erstwhile boyfriend.

The first time we meet Cal (Billy Zane's character in *Titanic*), who becomes the antagonist, he shows himself to be an arrogant, pompous aristocrat who treats servants as property and keeps his fiancée on a short leash. We dislike him within the first thirty seconds he's onscreen. That's a great character introduction.

Your secondary characters don't need as thorough an introduction as your protagonist, but they do merit careful thought for how you're going to bring them onstage the first time.

❧• REMEMBER THE IMPORTANCE OF FIRST IMPRESSIONS •❧

How will you introduce your main character? If you're starting the book with your protagonist onstage, you'll need to engage with action in addition to the other things we've talked about in this chapter. Not only will you need to reveal who your hero is at his core and how that is expressed in your specific story, you'll also need to package it in a scene that is interesting independent of anything you're doing with the main character.

So how will you do it? What's your hero's essential ingredient? We'll talk next about the other active ingredients that go into your character introduction. But by now you should be beginning to have some ideas not only for what needs to be done in that introduction but about how you might pull it off.

Think of your character introductions as short stories, little standalone short films created for the purpose of presenting your main characters to your reader. They will serve not only as introduction but as résumé and business card, brief snapshots conveying the essence of who these people are.

Most of the novelists I've worked with over the years do not naturally think to construct introductory short stories like this. They just want to get going with the main story, and they give almost no thought to how the reader will encounter the hero. But doing so with care is essential to get the protagonist "set" in the reader's mind. Watch some movies and see how the main characters are introduced. Then sit down and write a short story to introduce your hero.

Remember to show what is likable about your protagonist. That's where chapters four and five overlap—you engage your reader by introducing your hero in a way that shows what's heroic or sympathetic about her. Make us care about her.

First impressions are so powerful, especially in fiction. They shape every expectation we have about what this person is going to be like in the future. In a sense, they are deterministic *of* the future. In the character's introduction is the seed of the whole story. We see, in embryonic form, who he is, what makes him heroic, and where he is going.

CHAPTER 6

ESTABLISH YOUR HERO'S NORMAL

Every new beginning comes from some
other beginning's end. —SENECA

WOULD *TITANIC* WORK AS A MOVIE IF IT HAD BEGUN
as the ship was already sinking? Would *Close Encounters of the
Third Kind* have worked if it had started with the arrival of the
mother ship and the entry of our hero into it? Would *While You
Were Sleeping* have worked if it began with Lucy already fully acquainted with both Peter and Jack and the family?

The answer to all of these, in my opinion, is *probably not.*

If the ship were going down and we saw these characters running around chasing each other, it might be visually interesting,
but we would have no connection to these people, so we wouldn't
really care. If we saw random people filing into an alien spacecraft,
we'd be mildly interested, but it would have no emotional impact
on us. If we saw this young woman surrounded by a bunch of colorful characters, we might want to know more, but we would have
no ability to understand how all of this came to be.

A novel cannot start with the hero doing the most important
thing in the book. We'll talk about *in media res* beginnings in a future chapter, but even with books that begin in the middle of the

action or spend most of their time in flashback, you can't start at the climax, or the reader simply won't care. She will have no ability to connect with what's going on, and you will have squandered your story's most powerful moment.

Before you can be effective with what you want to do with your story, you have to set things up. You have to introduce the characters, establish the settings, lay out the stakes, and more.

You have to establish "normal" before you violate normal.

The *normal* is what things are like before the main action of the story intrudes. It's the "before" aspect of your book, to which the "after" will stand in contradistinction. We have to know the normal before we can comprehend how the main story represents a deviation from normal. It's the necessary setup you must do if you want your reader to be able to follow your tale.

I've put this chapter immediately after the chapter on how to introduce your main character because the topics are intertwined. Establishing normal includes more than the moment of the hero's first appearance, but the hero's normal and the story's normal have tremendous overlap, so it bears talking about them together.

❧· YOUR HERO'S NORMAL ·❧

What is your character like as the story begins—but before the main action of the story starts? What's he up to? Does he have a job? Is he going to school? Does he live on the streets or in a palace? Does he spend most of his time in the cow pasture or the dungeons or around the moons of Rigel 11?

What's he dealing with? A nosy mother? An insidious plague? A physical disability? What's his current situation? What's his daily life like? What are his challenges?

More importantly: What are his dreams? What's he aiming for? What hopes does he hold most dear? If he could have all power for one minute, what would he change about his life?

Remember, these are not things you will simply tell us about: "He lived with his grandmother but dreamed of becoming a forensic entomologist." These are things you will show us, things you will craft scenes to reveal to us.

In chapter eight we'll talk about your main character's inner journey and where on that path the story finds him at the outset. But right now I just want you to think about what your hero's normal, daily life is like when the curtain goes up.

You may well be answering many of these questions in the scene you write to introduce your hero, so pull out all those mental notes and begin jotting in the margin new ideas from this chapter. A great way to show your protagonist's essence is to show her doing her thing in her workaday life.

The first time we see the adult Lucy in *While You Were Sleeping*, she's sitting in her tollbooth collecting subway tolls and dreaming of love. Very soon after that, we see her in her tiny apartment alone with her cat.

The first time we see WALL-E, he's at work—alone in a vast city of trash, cleaning it up and playing with the things he finds. Soon after, he goes back to his home, and we see what his solitary life is like.

Are you detecting a trend here? Showing your hero's work and/ or home is a great way to establish her normal. The home or cubicle is a terrific place to pick all kinds of details to characterize this person. Think of Leonard and Sheldon's apartment in the TV show *The Big Bang Theory*. One glance at the action figures, movie replica props, classic science fiction movie posters, comic book collections, and high-end computer gear, and you know a lot about these people.

Pretend you're making a zoo for your main character. If you were creating a habitat to show her in her typical surroundings in her homeland, what elements would you include? Those are the things to include when you are writing the scenes that will establish her normal.

The first time we see Captain Jack Sparrow in *Pirates of the Caribbean: The Curse of the Black Pearl*, he is sailing a ship at sea. We expect it to be a sleek corsair slicing through the waves. Instead, it's a little dinghy that is literally sinking beneath his feet. As the ship sinks under the surface, Jack steps onto the dock. And, because there is no longer any ship, he doesn't have to pay the docking fee.

So what do we know about Jack's normal based on this scene? We know he can dress the part of a pirate, but we don't know if he is a true seaman. We know he has panache and a sea chest full of luck. We even get a sense of his character, that by choice or compulsion, he probably does a lot by relying on his luck. We see that he's a fast (if a little bizarre) talker and a shameless pickpocket. Before the end of his first page of lines, we know a lot about this character.

YOUR HERO'S HOME

Let's craft your protagonist's normal. Open a blank document on your computer or pull out a clean sheet of paper, and let's do some brainstorming.

Where does your hero live? Even if you never show this location in the novel, decide what her abode looks like. Where would this character live? Of course, where she would *like* to live and where she actually lives as the story begins may be two very different things. So describe them both.

By Darkness Hid by Jill Williamson begins with her hero living under the steps in the kitchen's cellars at the manor house of a minor lord. He ends up in a far different sort of abode, but that's how life is for him at the outset. That is his normal.

If your hero has the chance to decorate her residence, how would it be? Before Leonard becomes his roommate (in *The Big Bang Theory*), Sheldon had the apartment decorated in Early American Cardboard, complete with lawn chairs for furniture. What else could a person need? In *Scott Pilgrim vs. the World,* we see which things in the apartment belong to Scott and which to his roommate. (Scott has the cheesy, messy stuff; Wallace is responsible for the respectable décor.) Lars (Ryan Gosling's character in *Lars and the Real Girl*) lives in a mostly unfurnished garage attached to his brother's home. And have you ever seen a Sandra Bullock movie where you didn't see her apartment?

Showing your hero's home is a wonderful way to establish his normal. So what is your hero's home like? What kind of home is it? How many people live there? Is it nice or not so much? Is it in a good part of town? What's the general messiness level? What's on the wall (rock band posters, samurai swords, stuffed animal heads, old bowling shirts …)? What's in the closet? What's on the desk? What's the entertainment system, if any? What's in the fridge? What's in the backyard? Is the lawn mowed? What's on the front porch? What's in the garage? Are there any pets? What kind, how many, and in what state of health are they?

Of course, if this is a Western, a fantasy, a science fiction, or a story taking place in prehistoric times, these questions may be moot as I've posed them. But you can still figure out ways to establish your protagonist's normal by revealing what her home space is like.

It's true that you may never write a scene at your hero's house. That's okay. It's still important for you to know what it would be like. And if you do end up going there, you'll be set. Sometimes just the act of creating a place in this detail will have a way of imposing that place on your story. There will an almost gravitational force pulling you to have a scene there. Don't force one if it just wouldn't make sense for your story. But if it would make sense, don't fight it.

And if you can't write a scene in your hero's home, what about your hero's car? Or horse or spaceship or boat? One's personal mode of transportation is another great way to reveal the character's personality. To establish his normal.

YOUR HERO'S PLACE OF WORK

Most characters in most stories have a job. They do some kind of work, even if it's pushing a giant wheel around in a circle to grind grain, fighting as a soldier, or going to school. A few are vagrants, playboys, infants, or retirees, of course, but the chances are good that your hero will do some kind of labor every day. What is it?

Think of what job your character would be best at or would love. Depending on your story, he might even have that job. Forrest Gump had all kinds of jobs in his life, but the one he liked best was mowing the lawn for the city of Greenbow, Alabama. WALL-E seems mostly content to slowly clean up the city. He was (literally) made for that job. Dr. Alan Grant (Sam Neill's character in *Jurassic Park*) begins the story as an imminent paleontologist out on a dig. Sometimes it's best to show your hero doing what he's best-equipped to do.

Other times, it's better to show him doing something less than what his potential would allow, as we saw with Milo Thatch in *At-*

lantis. Achan, the boy sleeping under the stairs in *By Darkness Hid,* was made for ruling, not groveling, and yet that's not where he begins. Cinderella's situation is the classic beginning for a rags-to-riches tale.

What would it be for your hero? You've thought of her ideal job, but is that where she begins in this story? If not, what is her work as the curtain rises?

Your protagonist's job or workplace is a great source for revealing all sorts of things about who he is and what his situation is in your first fifty pages. What's his relationship with his boss? His co-workers? What does his workspace—cubicle, equipment cab, team locker, military post—look like? If he's had the opportunity to customize it to his liking, what has he done to the place?

YOUR HERO'S NORMAL SITUATION

Home and job are two of the biggies for showing your character's normal. That's where most characters spend most of their lives. But some characters are displaced or on a journey. And there are other aspects of a person's life besides these that should be revealed in the first fifty pages. As we go through them, write in your notes a couple of ideas for each category.

First, what are your main character's primary *relationships*? Is she single? Does he have kids? Is she living with her parents? Does he have a roommate? Who are the significant others in your protagonist's life? Does she hang out with her best friends from high school? Is there a bully in his life? Who are her allies and foes on an interpersonal level? Is there a girlfriend—or an ex, or more than one ex? Is anyone from work also a friend at home? Does she have any hangers-on? Fans? Stalkers? Interesting neighbors? Servants? Henchmen?

Your reader wants to know what your hero's life is like, and that includes the people (or creatures, sentient artificial intelligences, or invisible friends) in her circle. Often a friend character can serve as a powerful way to reveal something new about the main character, either by amplifying an aspect of the hero—showing where he could end up—or by contrasting an important facet of the hero— acting as a marvelous foil.

It may be that your story doesn't require you to reveal any of these people, or perhaps there *are* no others in the story (think *Cast Away* or *WALL-E*). But it at least bears thinking about. Most humans crave companionship, if only in the form of a pet roach or decorated volleyball. Chances are your hero does, too. Your main character's relationships are something that should be revealed in the first fifty pages.

As are your hero's *expectations*. An important part—possibly the most important part—of establishing the hero's normal is to show what her expectations are. Your task is to show us what her life is like and what she expects that life to be like for the foreseeable future. That sense of normalcy, that set of fixed conditions that constitute her regular life, is the still pond into which the story will drop a pebble. Or a meteorite.

Write down what your protagonist expects her next two weeks to be like. Assuming that everything else remains the same—as your characters are most likely doing—what will the next six months be like? The next three years? While you're at it, go ahead and project what she thinks her life will probably go like. If she were to cast her mind forward across her remaining years, what would she say there's a 75 percent chance of happening for her?

You're probably going to a throw a wrench into those gears with your story, but it's important to know, and to show to the reader, what her expectations are. It's only in the context of those assumptions that we can feel the full impact of the deviation from that course.

WALL-E clearly believes that the rest of his life will be spent making little cubes of trash and stacking them atop one another, with no end in sight and no one but a cockroach for a friend. Lightning McQueen in *Cars* (to choose another Pixar movie) assumes that he's destined to be the king of the Piston Cup racing circuit. Achan in *By Darkness Hid* believes he will be a stray (one step lower than a slave) for the rest of his life. Certainly Cinderella sees no end to her abuse.

Bruno (Asa Butterfield's character in *The Boy in the Striped Pajamas*) has to move from Berlin to the countryside because of his father's job with the military, but he sees no reason to believe his privileged life will ever be interrupted.

Into the lives of all these characters—including your hero's—some rain must fall. Indeed, your story is going to royally wreck those expectations. It's almost a sadistic sort of fun to fill your main character's head with these assumptions, knowing full well you're going to throw her a curve ball. Ah, the joy of being a novelist.

The third additional aspect of your hero's life to show your reader is his *hopes and dreams*. His expectations might be pretty bleak, but he yearns for more. One day, his ship will come in. One day, her fairy godmother will appear. One day, he'll leave all this behind.

What does your protagonist hope to achieve? If she could have three wishes, what would they be? If he is trying to better himself or improve his condition, how is he going about it?

One of your main tasks in your first fifty pages is to make your reader engage with your hero. An excellent way to do that is to show us what she's longing to become, especially if it looks like she'll never achieve it. We pull for the underdog. We root for the plucky kid with a dream and the gumption to go for it. Because we ourselves dream, and we know what it is to be foiled. And sometimes seeing a character gather the courage to attempt something is the motivation we need to go for our own dream.

What is your hero hoping for? How is she pursuing that dream? How likely does it seem that dream might be? Write down a few ideas.

Is she sitting in her forest home singing about when her prince will come and sweep her away? Is he down at the gym seven days a week working on that free throw? Is she learning Mandarin in hopes of moving to China to work with orphans? Is he taking night classes to earn a degree in restaurant management?

Do you see how the showing—as opposed to telling—ways of revealing your hero's dream are suggesting themselves? You don't have to say, "She longed to be a chef." Instead, you have her playing and replaying a DVD of a cooking show while she works feverishly to create what she's watching. You don't have to say, "He wanted to be a movie star." No, you'd have him going from audition to audition, perhaps moving from feature film auditions to auditions for off-off-Broadway productions, to auditions for toothpaste commercials, his posture slumping more as he leaves each one. Okay, that's a detour, but everything goes back to craft.

WHAT WAS THE QUESTION?

There is a power in your hero's dreams that may not be immediately evident. What your protagonist longs for, as in her dearest dream and most active hope (even if she's not aware of it herself), is the basis of that high-sounding term, the *story question*.

The story question sounds mysterious and profound, but it's quite simple. It just means *will the hero get what he's hoping for?*

If your hero dreams of finding love, will she find it? In this novel, I mean. If your hero longs for adventure, will he have an adventure? Go all psychological, too. Peer deeply into your main character's psyche. If what she's really yearning for is not to be a chef, as her behavior would suggest, but to please her mother, is that something she's going to be able to do in this book? Manny the mammoth wants to be left alone, but what he really wants is to have a family to care for again. Whether or not he can find that place in the universe is the story question.

So what is your protagonist's story question? What is it he wants … and will he get it?

Jot down five or six ways her true desire can be expressed, and then five or six ways it could be fulfilled. Then think about whether or not you're going to let her have her dream.

A powerful tool in fiction is to reveal your hero's "hole" and then flirt with filling it or leaving it, as it were, unfulfilled. Your reader feels the pull of that vacuum and wants it to be satisfied. It's up to you to do so or not, but understanding that this dynamic is at work will equip you to manage reader expectations and hopes.

As you toy with them (er, as you manage reader expectations), you increase suspense. I call it the Jane Austen effect. Make 'em think the hero and heroine will never be allowed to get together. Right up to the very end. Your readers will love hating the angst you give them. For a great example of this, watch *The Wedding Singer.* If you do this, though, you'd best let the story question be answered in the affirmative, or your reader will be ticked.

Will your hero achieve her deepest hope? That, my friend, is the (story) question.

❧ MAKE US FEEL IT ❧

In order for your reader to feel afraid for Jack and Rose when the *Titanic* begins to sink, you'd better have introduced us to them, shown us their relationship, and revealed their dreams. Then when the deck is tilting and the hull is filling with water and our hero is handcuffed to the pipe and the villain is coming with a gun … we'll feel it. Oh, baby, we'll feel it.

When Roy Neary and the others don their space gear and march into the mother ship in *Close Encounters of the Third Kind*, we'd better know him and how's he's driven and what he's been through, or we won't care that he's leaving Earth possibly forever. But if he's become our friend, you bet we'll care.

If we've seen Lucy from *While You Were Sleeping* alone in her pathetic apartment with her cat and working alone in her tollbooth on Christmas because she's the only employee with no family, we'll definitely rejoice to see her with a surrogate family. When she's surrounded by crazy relatives and favorite uncles and handsome suitors, we feel her joy right alongside her. But if we hadn't seen what came before, we would have no way of understanding the change, and our empathy for her would be nil.

Show us your hero's normal. Establish for us what his life is like before the main action of the story invades. It's the only way to make your reader fully connect with what you're doing. You want your reader to feel the impact of your story and the transformation and travail the hero undergoes. We can't comprehend his "after" until you've shown us his "before."

What is your protagonist's normal, and how can you show that onstage?

CHAPTER 7

ESTABLISH YOUR STORY WORLD'S NORMAL

*All great deeds and all great thoughts have a ridiculous beginning.
Great works are often born on a street corner or in a restaurant's revolving door.*
—ALBERT CAMUS

IN CHAPTER THREE I SAID POLITE CONVERSATION requires that we explain things before we tell a story, but that in fiction we don't do that. I said that when we're verbally relating a tale to someone, we first give them some background information so that when the key part of the story happens, the listener isn't tripped up wondering what it all means. You will have put the background information in the listener's mind, thus avoiding confusion at the crucial moment.

Then I talked about how good fiction craftsmanship is counterintuitive on this point, because outright explaining is *telling*, which will likely get your book rejected. What you ought to do is *show*, I said, which is less like exposition and more like cinema.

All true. Good stuff.

In this chapter I'm going to sound like I'm disagreeing with myself. But I'm not. Don't worry, it will all make sense soon.

WAIT, ISN'T THIS TELLING?

In the tactical, fiction craftsmanship sense, we should not come right out and explain things to the reader. "Joey was a slob." It's mind-numbing and amateurish and, some would say, lazy writing.

But in the strategic sense, we must convey information to the reader so he will be able to understand what's happening. As we saw in the previous chapter, an awareness of what is happening now is a prerequisite for the comprehension of what happens later.

So which is it, Jeff? Do I explain things for the reader or not? You said the first fifty pages are not the place for explanation, and yet here you've devoted two chapters to explaining things in the first fifty pages!

Um … yes. Sorry for the confusion. Let's sort it out.

We're talking about two kinds of information—and two methods for delivering it. For the *kind* of information, the key is whether or not the reader needs to know it. For the *method* of delivery, the issue is how the reader gets the information.

If you stop the story to explain something the reader doesn't need to know, you're telling. Telling is a Bad Thing. But that doesn't mean there is no information the reader needs to know. If your story is about tornado chasers, the reader needs to know what an F-5 Tornado is. If your story is about computer hackers, the reader needs to know a bit about how hacking is done. The challenge isn't to write a story that requires no information to be transmitted to the reader, but to transmit the necessary information in a way that does not stop the story, bore the reader, or get your book rejected.

Showing, then, is about carefully selecting what information must be conveyed to the reader and then conveying it in an interesting way. The criterion is that the selected information must be conveyed or the reader will not understand what's going on.

When I talk about establishing normal, I'm talking about a category of information that meets the condition: It is information that must be conveyed to the reader or there will be confusion.

I read an unpublished manuscript once in which, on page 1, a character is walking along a street and is blown by a mysterious wind into a shop and sent to an alternate dimension. But because this was page 1, I had no clue what this person's life was like or even what this person's world was like. As far as I knew, mysterious winds were the primary means of transportation in this world. And as far as I could tell, this person got blown to alternate dimensions six or eight times a day.

Without context, we have no way of gauging how the action of the story is unusual. Before we can grasp that the mysterious wind is, in fact, mysterious, we have to first perceive that this person's life does not regularly include such winds.

So this information must be conveyed to the reader. It meets the condition. Now, you wouldn't do it by saying, "In Carlotta's world, mysterious winds do not typically blow, nor are alternate dimensions something that constitute Carlotta's everyday life." Ack, no. That would be telling. What you'd do is work with action, dialogue, and scene—probably a full scene, in this case—to *show* the reader what Carlotta's life, world, and expectations are.

Then, when the wind blows and the portal opens, the reader will deduce that those are abnormal events.

Telling is when you stop the story to explain something the reader doesn't need to know and doesn't care about. Establishing normal is when you use cinematic techniques to show the reader some information she must know in order to feel the impact when the story comes along and changes the hero's life.

There *is* information that must be conveyed to the reader before the main action of the story can begin. It just has to be conveyed through showing.

✥· WHY ESTABLISH NORMAL? ·✥

You've probably surmised the reasons by now. We establish normal in order to show how the events of the story are a deviation from the way things had been. This allows us to feel the impact the deviation has on the hero and her world.

So why a full section explaining why to establish normal? Because I work with countless writers who don't establish normal before violating normal. Because I work with thousands of writers conference attendees who don't establish normal before violating normal. And because when I explain to them why you must first establish normal, I get this particular blank look. Or they'll nod sagely and write it down in their notes, but when I read their stories they will have begun with the main action of the story intruding on page 1.

You can't begin the main action of the story on page 1 of your book. It doesn't work.

I perceive that what I'm saying is harder to get across than I had at first imagined. Writers may feel the urgency to begin their books with action, so they begin with the *main* action. That this is a mistake that sabotages the very thing they're trying to do must not be immediately evident. And so I risk beating a dead horse to be sure I've well and truly made my case.

THE IMPORTANCE OF BEING NORMAL

Before Arthur pulled Excalibur from the stone (in *Excalibur*), we saw what his life was like as a squire and a young man in medieval England. We'd even seen other men—stronger and more mature—try to pull the sword from the stone and fail. But imagine if, instead of starting that way, the movie had begun with Arthur pulling Excalibur from the rock. Right there in the opening shot of the film. If it had begun like that, we'd have no understanding of how hard it was to pull it out and how becoming king marked a change for him.

In *The Hunt for Red October* we saw Jack Ryan's life as family man and quiet analyst for the CIA. We saw that he was quite comfortable in his little cubicle back home. The guy didn't even know how to make a decent PowerPoint presentation to a committee. When he gets sent into the theater of action to try to prevent World War III, we perceive that combat helicopters, aircraft carriers, and shootouts in nuclear attack subs are not exactly his usual fare. But if we hadn't seen him until he was aboard a military submarine, we would have had no clue how out of water this fish really was.

The first time we see Josie Geller in *Never Been Kissed*, she's a frumpy, forgettable young copyeditor at a newspaper. During the course of the movie, she goes back to high school as an undercover reporter and becomes one of the popular kids. Now, if the movie had begun with her as a popular kid, we would not feel how much of a change this was in her life.

Fletcher Reede (Jim Carrey's character in *Liar Liar*) lies as a matter of course. Whatever he needs to say to get ahead, he says. He lies to his mother, his co-workers, his ex-wife, and, to a degree, even to his young son. But then something happens that causes him to be incapable of telling a lie. The result is hysterical hijinks as he is forced to use something besides falsehoods to get through his life.

Imagine if we'd had no setup. Imagine if on page 1 of the script he'd been told he could not lie? The fun of the movie would be gone. We wouldn't have known the despicableness of this no-good liar if we hadn't seen him being just that. We wouldn't rejoice as he gets his comeuppance if we hadn't seen him earn it. We wouldn't yearn for him to be kind to the people around him if we hadn't seen him hurt them.

In your novel, you are going to change your hero's life. Something is coming into her world that will send her careening down a path she'd never wanted to explore. But in order for readers to realize just how odd this change is—and just how *needed* this change is—you must show them what her life was like before the change came.

A gladiator whom we have not seen as a decorated Roman general is, in the end, just a gladiator. A princess whom we have not seen as an abused stepchild is just a princess. A handsome young man whom we have not seen as an ugly green ogre is just a handsome young man. A wizard whom we have not seen as an unwanted child forced to live in a stairwell closet is, in the reader's eyes, just another wizard.

If you want us to feel the things you want us to feel about your story, you have to give us the setup. You have to show what life was like for the hero before the change came.

Before you can violate normal, you have to establish what that normal was.

When you turn to your novel, please don't begin with the main action of the story intruding into the hero's world—unless it is your goal for the reader to not care about your story. I suspect that's not why you've decided to write a novel. So allow the reader to engage. Show him the state of things as they were on the eve of the Big Change that is your main story. Then you can begin the fireworks.

❧ THE STORY WORLD'S NORMAL ❧

In chapter six we looked at establishing the hero's normal. We explored ideas for her home and job and primary relationships. If the best fiction is a blend of character transformation and an intriguing plot that amplifies the character's change, as I argue in *Plot Versus Character*, understanding the hero's condition before the change begins is paramount to the novel.

For the remainder of this chapter we're going to look at establishing the normal of the story world before the main action of the book gets going. I've got more to say about the things you need to establish about the protagonist in the first fifty pages, which we'll get to in chapter eight. But since we were already talking about establishing normal for the hero, it makes sense to complete that topic before moving on.

Some of our task here is to show what conditions the story world is experiencing now, conditions that will be reshaped during the course of the book. For instance, showing what Marty McFly's hometown looked like in 1955 vs. how it looked in 1985 (*Back to the Future*).

The rest of our work in establishing normal in the story world is to reveal the novel's genre, milieu, era, setting, backdrop, and tone.

You may not have realized how much a writer has to accomplish in the first fifty pages of a novel. I'd taught this material in conferences and with clients for years, but when I sat down to write it into book form, I was surprised at just how much we do in those opening spreads. The good news is that it's almost easier to do it than to talk about doing it. I might take a page to talk about establishing a book's genre, but you can do it in your novel just by having someone zoom up in a spaceship.

❧· SETTING US UP FOR A CHANGE ·❧

Probably the largest part of showing what a story's normal is consists of showing what the *hero's* normal is. But sometimes the world itself is set to be altered. In order for us to understand that change, we have to see what it was like before it happened.

Disney's *The Lion King* shows the African savannah when Mufasa ruled it. The land was colorful, sumptuous, and full of life. But when Scar usurps the throne and brings in his own style of leadership, the land suffers. The colors go from vibrant to dark and grey. The vigorous flora shrivels to dead twigs. The flourishing cornucopia of life becomes a wasteland.

If the story had started in the latter condition, we would have no measure for comprehending how far things had fallen.

A clear before-and-after tale in which the story world changes is *The Matrix*. Neo's world is the world at the end of the twentieth century. But in reality, it's hundreds of years later and exists only as a desolate pile of ruins. But if the movie had started in the wasteland, we would've felt no surprise or wonder when we saw it. It was only in the contrast between what the hero thought and what he discovered that the impact became pronounced.

In *Kate & Leopold*, a character from the 1800s is transported to the twenty-first century. We'd seen him in his natural habitat—as an aristocrat in New England—before the change. If he'd just been walking around modern-day Central Park the first time we saw him, it would've had much less power. But to see what his world was like before the change … that was cool.

Same with Giselle in *Enchanted*. Her "before" world was actually a two-dimensional animated land that seemed more Disney than Disney. She gets thrust into our real world, and her adventure begins. But if the movie had started as she climbed out of a manhole in downtown New York, it wouldn't have struck us as it did. By showing what her world had been like before, we felt her fear and confusion as she walked around in our reality.

In your first fifty pages, you need to set up how things were before the main story began. Maybe the landscape itself is going to be altered, and maybe it isn't. But it will behoove you to give thought to what elements of the story world at the outset may stand in contrast to those same elements later.

Establish normal before you violate normal.

❧ GENRE, MILIEU, ERA, SETTING, BACKDROP, AND TONE ❧

Part of establishing your story world for your readers in the first fifty pages is to let them know what kind of book this is going to be. Is it going to be a Western? A police procedural? A romantic comedy? And not only genre, but what time and place this novel is going to take place in, and what will be its tone?

In many ways, the classic example of how to begin a story right is the opening sequence of *Raiders of the Lost Ark*. Through that set of scenes in the jungle we learn that this character is a man of action who is knowledgeable about ancient tricks and traps. We learn that this is going to be an action-adventure story. We learn that it's taking place in 1936, which has its own set of implications. We learn that it's probably not going to take place mostly indoors, like in someone's comfy office somewhere. We even get a sense for the almost comic tone the story is going to have.

As you contemplate how you're going to open your novel, keep in mind that you need to reveal these things as well. Most are easily done, but it's also possible to overlook them and end up confusing your reader. So they are worth looking at one by one.

GENRE

What is your book's genre? Is it science fiction or historical or urban fantasy? Now, there's nothing that says your book has to be genre fiction. You may intentionally eschew such categories. That's fine. But even so, you'll need to let your reader know what sort of book this is going to be.

Basically, you need to let us in on the rules. If the climax of your book is going to consist of the hero getting into a time machine and jumping away to safety, we had better have known in the first fifty pages that time travel is possible in the world of your story.

This touches on the topic I call *plant and payoff*. It's a mixed metaphor, I know, but I like the alliteration. The *plant* is when you establish something, like that time travel is possible. The *payoff* is when you use time travel later in the story. In the first fifty pages, you're doing a lot of planting. You're letting us know all kinds of things about your characters and story world that will be used later. Plant away, O gardener!

Just be sure there is a payoff to every plant and a plant to every payoff. Don't let your hero suddenly know how to do brain surgery in the book's climax if you haven't established (planted) beforehand that he could do this. And don't plant that he can do brain surgery if you're not going to let him do it later on. Don't make your reader notice things that aren't important—unless you're writing a mystery, but I digress.

Letting us know the genre of your book is a good shorthand way to let us know the rules. If you show a guy walking around with a couple of six-shooters and boots and a cowboy hat, we're going to think this is a Western. If you show a woman in the garb of English ladies circa 1815, especially if she's playing coquette with a wounded warrior from the Napoleonic wars, we're going to think this is a Regency romance. A squad of American soldiers walking warily through the hedgerows of the French countryside is going to make us think this is a war novel.

I point this out because it is possible to unintentionally mislead your reader. You might begin with a playful scene between a man and a woman who are clearly flirting with one another. You might put them in an ambiguous setting, like a beach or a field, so we don't get any clues about genre. Their language and behavior and morals might suggest a modern story—or something else entirely. Then when the scene changes and we see this is horror fiction set in the Middle Ages, it's going to give us a jolt, but not the kind of jolt you were hoping for.

Help your reader out. Just trot out a half-goblin in chainmail armor and a shield if this is a fantasy. Have someone make an arrest if this is a police story. Send in the clones. Part of your job in the first fifty pages is to orient your reader into what kind of story this is going to be.

MILIEU, ERA, AND SETTING

Even if your novel is not genre fiction, it is surely going to happen in a specific time and place. This isn't the place to discuss these at length, but I will suggest that you play around with different choices to see if one might do a better job of achieving your objectives than the one you'd originally had in mind.

Whatever milieu you choose for your story, establish it in your first fifty pages. If this is a novel set in the American frontier in the latter half of the nineteenth century, be sure to show a covered wagon and someone churning butter. If it's taking place on the fourteenth moon of Beta-Trigocide, show us a spaceship and an alien or two. If it's happening in modern-day Beijing, show us a rickshaw going through a back alley to a hutong. Show us Chinese people. Throw us a rope.

You need to convey to us in the first fifty pages—and the first five pages, preferably—not only *when* this story is taking place but *where*. Where in the sense of whether it's someone's house or an office building, but also where in the sense of what town or city, what kind of terrain in the region, and what nation or culture. Establishing normal is all about context.

Geography and level of technology and population density. Whether the place is well-kept or run-down. Whether a yellow sun presides in a blue sky, or three green suns in a purple sky. Urban desolation or Garden of Eden.

Some stories can work well in a number of milieus. Consider *Three Amigos*, *A Bug's Life*, and *Galaxy Quest*, which are all basically the same story—actors are mistaken for the real thing and must decide to stop pretending in order to save the innocents who believed in them. But the choice of era, setting, and even genre allow you to enhance your story and give it the precise feeling you're wanting.

How do movies establish milieu, era, and setting? Usually by having a 1950s-era car drive by, showing a dragon circling a wizard's tower, or showing a teen walk by with an iPad X stuck under his nose.

You can do it the same way. Think like a filmmaker when it comes to establishing the normal of your story world. How would you clue in an audience that this novel is going to take place under the polar ice cap in 2211? Flex that good fiction lobe in your brain. Put it in front of the camera.

BACKDROP

Some stories take place in the shadow of a larger event like war, famine, disaster, or a movement of some kind. What would *The Untouchables* be without Prohibition? What would *The Dirty Doz-*

en be without World War II? What would *The Right Stuff* be without the space race?

I'd like to again suggest that you consider choosing a backdrop for your novel. Sometimes your topic forces you to use a specific backdrop—like *The Untouchables* and *The Right Stuff*, because they are dramatizations of real events. But other times you are free to choose any backdrop you like ... so choose one that helps you tell your story. You might not have thought of it, and maybe you'll end up not selecting one, but it's worth expending a bit of brain juice on it to see if something might underline what you want to do with your novel.

Maybe you want to write a love story about a woman from a monied family longing to leave those things behind and live free but who is prevented from doing so by an aristocratic system and a controlling fiancé. Great. Whatever setting you choose for that will probably be very interesting. But why not set it on the *Titanic*?

A backdrop will carry with it certain expectations and moods—and, as here, sometimes a backdrop will even come with a looming deadline to increase suspense.

A boy's discovery of the cruelty man can inflict on innocents would work well in any of a variety of settings and genres. But certain backdrops could lend the story a flavor you're looking for, as we learned in the unforgettable *The Boy in the Striped Pajamas*, which is set against the concentration camps of World War II.

What power could you add to your story if you told it in the muddy fields of Woodstock—or the muddy fields of the Battle of Bannockburn? Would your hero's transformation be more powerful if she were the fiancée of a man headed to the Alamo in Texas's war for independence? What if your protagonist had just gotten a job in one of the World Trade Center towers on September 1, 2001?

They don't have to be real events, either. If you're created a make-believe world, you can also create famines or invasions or epidemics or whatever you want. In that case, I would almost always recommend choosing some backdrop that will underline the themes you're wanting to examine in the book.

If you do choose a backdrop, you need to reveal it in the first fifty pages. Or at least give clues, if you have reason to keep it concealed. Your reader probably shouldn't be shocked to find out at the climax of the book that the hero is living in Kesennuma City, Japan, just as the tsunami hits.

Part of your job of establishing normal in your story world is to let the reader know what backdrop the story is playing out against. Reveal it cinematically, but do reveal it—in the first fifty pages.

TONE

The last aspect of establishing the normal of your story is to set the tone.

Occasionally I read unpublished manuscripts that mislead the reader as to the book's tone. The author hasn't meant to do so. Probably he started writing it when he was in one mood and figured out as he went that what he really wanted to write was this other kind of story over here. You need to work to be sure your tone is consistent and is what you're intending.

By *tone* I mean the novel's sense of seriousness, humor, or irony. Mood and flavor. Contrast the tone of *Down With Love* with that of *Apocalypse Now*. Contrast *Wag the Dog* with *The Bourne Identity*. Contrast *Grease* with *West Side Story*.

You may not even realize you're creating a tone for your novel, but you are. It has to do with voice, message, and theme, but mainly it's the feeling you give the story. Your novel's tone might be gritty or snarky, playful or alarmist, political or optimistic. Or something else entirely.

Whatever it is, you need to establish it in the first fifty pages.

A novel that begins with horrific multiple murders had better not be a musical comedy, you know what I'm saying? Or vice versa. What if *Raiders of the Lost Ark* had started as it does but then been a dry courtroom drama for the rest of it? What if *Lawrence of Arabia* had been about a British soldier who trekked across the desert by camel and then took up a career as a stand-up comedian?

The tone you set in your first fifty pages must be the tone you want for the whole book. With this and so much else in this book, you always want to be building your ending into your beginning. So think carefully about what tone you want, and write accordingly. Then maybe have someone else read over what you have so far to be sure you're achieving the right tone.

Here's a tip: Find music that puts you in the mood you want the reader to be in when she reads your book, and have that music playing when you write your first fifty pages. If you're riding the wave of that perfect music while you're pounding out the words, you've got a much higher probability of creating the tone you want.

❧· GET READY ·❧

The Pixar film *WALL-E* is, in my opinion, a modern classic. It's hugely enjoyable as a movie, and the hero is irresistible. If you want a great lesson on how to reveal a ton of information without a lick of telling, watch the first twenty minutes of this movie.

WALL-E is brilliant storytelling, and not least in how it begins.

Think about how it establishes normal, both in terms of the hero's "before" life and in terms of the story world before the main action of the story intrudes. We see WALL-E's daily life. We see his work. We see his home. We see the surroundings he finds himself in, including not only how desolate it is but that he is so alone.

Through the hero's actions, we get a feel for his playful, child-like character and also for the tone of the movie. The backdrop is an Earth so clogged with garbage and commercialism that it's no longer able to sustain organic life.

By the time the main story invades his world—in the form of an automated probe coming down on a periodic patrol to scan for life—we feel firmly situated in WALL-E's milieu. We know his expectations, relationships, and goals.

We are, in a word, ready.

We're ready for the story. We're ready for the major disruption that will come into his life. We're primed. Set up. When that disruption arrives, we understand instantly how it impacts our hero—and how it is drastically different from what has come before. It's thrilling and frightening (in the suspenseful way the filmmakers are shooting for), and whatever our little guy chooses to do, we're with him.

That's what you're after in your first fifty pages. You need to so establish normal for your hero and his world that when the story throws him a curve, we're ready, too. We're ready for the change. We're ready for an adventure. And we're with your hero, come what may.

In fiction, you don't want to stop your story to explain things. But you do have information you need readers to know if you want them to be able to resonate with what happens in your novel. Using the tools of the filmmaker to reveal these things, set your readers up by establishing normal. When it's well and truly set up, you can drop your bomb into it. And then the fun can really begin.

CHAPTER 8
START THE INNER JOURNEY

A journey of a thousand miles must begin with a single step. **–LAO-TZU**

GRU IS DESPICABLE. HE IS A VILLAIN. HE MAKES CHILDREN cry for the fun of it. He uses his freeze ray to cut to the front of the line at Starbucks. He has legions of minions who help him pull off dastardly crimes and become the world's worst villain. To top it off, he threatens to kill his neighbor's pooch.

Gru is also in for the ride of his life. Something is about to come into his carefully structured world and send him hurtling in a direction he would never have predicted.

The writers of *Despicable Me* understood that the best fictional stories have at the heart of them the transformation of the central character.

Survey your favorite stories, be they novels or movies or plays. My hunch is that most of them are ultimately about a character undergoing a change. *Star Wars, Gone With the Wind, Citizen Kane, Casablanca, Lawrence of Arabia, Groundhog Day, It's a Wonderful Life, Schindler's List, Apocalypse Now,* and most of the greatest stories of all time focus on the hero starting as one thing and becoming something else.

It is our joy to watch the events of a story come along and "assist" the hero to make this change. I think this resonates with us because we are constantly on our way to becoming something new, so we enjoy stories that let us watch other people navigate their change.

Of course there are purely plot-driven stories in which the hero does not change but merely reacts (like *Blade Runner, North by Northwest*, or any Indiana Jones or James Bond movie). And there is a whole class of story that involves a main character who is already so perfected that everyone else must change around that person (think *Mary Poppins, WALL-E, Forrest Gump, E.T., Anne of Green Gables,* and Jesus Christ).

But so long as you're strategizing your novel, why not plan to give your hero a compelling inner journey? If you can craft a great character arc and wrap a suspenseful story around it, keeping both plot and character in balance, you will have achieved the Holy Grail of fiction writing, and your novel will be much more attractive to agents, editors, and readers.

❧· OVERVIEW OF THE INNER JOURNEY ·❧

A character who is ripe for an inner journey is a character who has something inside her that needs to be changed. She's living out of balance with herself, even if she doesn't realize it. And the universe is going to conspire to rectify her situation.

Gru is a villain, but he's really not. He knows each of his minions by name, he (secretly) has a heart for children, and all he really wants is for his mom to be proud of him. His true self is something nonvillainous, but he's living in denial of that fact. So the story is going to make sure he gets this dilemma worked out.

Josie Geller (Drew Barrymore's character in *Never Been Kissed*) has always wanted to be popular, and now she's getting her chance. She's beginning to detect all the shallowness involved in the clique life. She's even taking part in it, which causes her to lose friends among the unpopular group. In the pursuit of what had always been denied her, she's trying to be something she's not, and it's eating her up inside. The story is going to help her find her true self.

One of the most famous inner journeys is that of Anakin Skywalker/Darth Vader in the *Star Wars* movies. He began as a plucky little kid with a heart of gold. But events, people, and his own choices caused him to go down a dark road and become one of the most iconic villains of our culture. And yet this was not who he really was. He'd never wanted to go there. So the universe (the Force?) brings about events that will remind him of who he is at his core and will give him the chance to become that person again.

Alex Fletcher (Hugh Grant's character in *Music and Lyrics*) is so out of touch with the soulful composer he really is that it's just comical. Sad, but comical. He's playing Knott's Berry Farm and trying to cash in on his fading glory as a pop star from yesteryear. At the beginning of the movie, he's desperately hoping to get on a new TV show called *Battle of the Eighties Has-Beens*. It's pathetic, and the story is not going to let him stay in that situation any longer.

Likewise, in *Galaxy Quest*, Alexander Dane (Alan Rickman's character) has become numb to his life. He was a Shakespearean actor who received three curtain calls for his portrayal of Richard III. But now he's going from science fiction convention to science fiction convention, eking out a living as a washed-up star of a cancelled TV show. His low point comes when he's asked to convert his character's most famous line to be more suitable for an electronics store opening: "By Grabthar's hammer, what a savings." The story is going to help him find meaning in his life and work again.

The key to a good transformation story is that, at the outset, the hero is trying to play against her own destiny or true self. The result is a character out of balance. Which usually means *miserable*.

What could that be for your protagonist? Throughout this chapter, keep going back to your hero. You've done your character work, so you know who he is at his core. But at the beginning of *this* story, who is he? Is there some repressed desire that needs to come out? Is he in a relationship he really shouldn't be in? Is he trying to be something he really isn't? Look for a way to place him in a situation that causes him internal conflict.

Choose carefully, of course, because the undoing of that imbalance is going to be what the bulk of your story is about.

In fiction, a great inner journey begins with a character in need of a significant change. That's Point A. The journey then leads directly to her moment of truth, that instant when she realizes how she's out of balance and must decide, once and for all, whether she's going to stay with the imbalance or make the change that will lead to her regaining her true self.

This moment of truth comes to Darth Vader when he sees his son being attacked by the Emperor. All the good aspects of his character, the remnants of that gold-hearted boy from long ago, call him to intervene to save his son from death. But he's invested so much in the dark side of the Force that he almost can't hear those aspects anymore—and if he turns on his master, it will surely cost him his life. Ah, beautiful angst!

Your job as novelist is to get your hero to that very same precipice. That is the destination and the *purpose* of an inner journey. Show her how she's not being true to who she really wants to be, make the choice cost her dearly no matter what she chooses, and then step back and see what she does.

The inner journey is primarily about your hero's imbalance (in *Plot Versus Character,* I refer to it as the hero's *knot* that must be untied), which is Point A, and getting him to his moment of truth where he can decide to return to his true self or plunge more deeply into the imbalance he's been living, which is Point B. Everything else is support for that A-to-B journey.

Let's look at the mile markers on this trail.

First, we need to see him in his unbalanced situation. This is his *initial condition.* Because this is how the character is in the first fifty pages of the novel, we'll be talking about initial condition in this chapter.

Next is the thing that sends her off onto the detour that will ultimately lead to her moment of truth. This is the *inciting event.* Alex Fletcher's inciting event is when some woman who wasn't even supposed to be there walks into his apartment to water his plants and, almost without thinking, begins supplying brilliant lyrics for the song he's writing. This is the fateful moment that will eventually result in Alex having the chance to return to who he is at his core.

The inciting event will also happen in the first fifty pages of your novel, so we'll discuss it at length in this chapter as well.

Between the inciting event and the moment of truth is the *escalation.* This is the internal struggle in which the hero tries to hold onto his old, unbalanced way of living while the new alternative begins presenting itself as, to quote a line from *Music and Lyrics,* a way back into love. During the escalation, your hero will be pushed and pressed and knocked about because she refuses to embrace the change that will result in her inner healing. This is the force the story brings. It is the press of Fate, the very hand of God, increasing pressure on her to admit that her old way is hurting her and the new way ought to at least be considered.

The culmination of the escalation is the *moment of truth*. That is the singular moment when the hero decides what to do about the imbalance inside him. He understands that he's not being true to himself, and he acknowledges that something must change. The only choice remaining is whether to leave the harmful way forever or to stop being halfhearted about it and give himself to it utterly.

He's been on the fence, and it's been hurting. The story has come along and set the fence on fire. He is going to jump off of it; you as the storyteller have left him no choice in that matter and no more time to delay the decision. The only question is, which direction will he jump? Will Darth Vader fully embrace the dark side and thus sacrifice his son—and what remains of his soul—or will he choose a path that will result in his own destruction but will be true to his all-but-forgotten core self?

The whole point of writing a novel, it can be argued, is to show a character's transformation. And the whole point of writing a character's transformation is to get him to his moment of truth.

After the moment of truth, the only part of the inner journey remaining is the *final state*. This is what your hero has become as a result of what she chose at her moment of truth.

In most stories, the hero will choose the "right" option, the path that leads back to who he really is. So Alex Fletcher leaves the eighties has-been scene behind and returns to composing from the heart. Josie Geller throws off the prom queen crown and goes back to being a person of substance (not that we can't have prom queens of substance; I'm just sayin' …). Alexander Dane realizes there is nobility in acting, and he gives his Shakespearean best to his TV role. Gru embraces his paternal side and goes from villain to hero, which is what he'd always been deep inside but had just tried to forget.

Note that the final state and the initial condition are joined at the hip. If your hero's initial condition is that she's tried to say she does not want to be a mother, despite the fact that you know that's what she yearns for, her final condition can be one of only two things: Either she's become a mother in some sense or she has removed all possibility of motherhood from her future.

Your hero's final state is either the opposite of the imbalance she started with or it is that imbalance times ten. At the moment of truth, she will choose the way back into love … or she will embrace madness and fling herself into the abyss. Literarily speaking.

Your hero's inner journey is like a wildfire that chases him to the end of a pier. Like it or not, he must make a choice. He can make a leap for the last boat out, or he can choose to stay and be consumed. The fire began in his own heart because he tried to live in a way that was not in harmony with what he really wanted and who he really is. But the fire got out of control, and now he has to leave behind everything he's grown accustomed to—including the falsehood that kindled the flame in the first place—or he has to choose to let it destroy him.

It doesn't have to be that melodramatic, of course. Chick-lit and scatological comedies can and should have compelling inner journeys, and these don't have to involve plunging into madness or an abyss of fire. But the milestones on the journey are the same, if not quite so incendiary.

❧ IMBALANCING THE BOOKS ❧

In the first fifty pages of your novel, the inner journey will begin, so we need to study certain parts of it in more detail.

The hero's knot (the imbalance) is in full effect in his life. This imbalance results in the initial condition, which is a depiction of what the knot is doing to him as the story opens. Then along will come a little kick in the keister, the inciting event, which is an unwanted interruption that heralds the arrival of the way of balance. Depending on your story, your first fifty pages may even include portions of the escalation phase. And certainly the seeds of your protagonist's final state are planted in these opening spreads.

Let's begin with your hero's knot. If you're going to create an inner journey for your protagonist, and I urge you to do so, figure out what her issue is. What's her deal? What's her problem? In what way is she trying to convince herself that living contrary to her true character is the right thing to do?

A good knot reverberates all the way down to the level of the psyche. To that part of the brain that responds when you look at a Rorschach test. "He's hungry" would not be a good knot, for instance, nor would "He's trying to convince himself that he's not hungry." You have to go deeper, even if you're writing a light comedy.

For instance, in *Three Amigos* all three of our movie stars are not living in reality. They're prissy and convinced of their own superiority and removed from the rigors of the real world. They're not mature men. More like spoiled babies. There is true heroism inside them, but they haven't found it yet. They haven't had to. The story will come along and force them to choose between being heroes or continuing to only pretend to be heroes. Their knot, then, would be that they've convinced themselves that ersatz heroism is enough.

So it's not exactly *King Lear*. But it is the basis for a great character arc.

Evan Baxter (Steve Carell's character in *Evan Almighty*) is shallow and flippant. He's been elected to the Senate, but he's more interested in having a nice office than fulfilling his campaign promise to change the world. Evan's life has very little meaning outside of pleasing Evan. That's his knot: He's self-centered and content to just coast along at the surface. But the story god—or in this case, literally God—loves him too much to leave him in that condition. And so he is prevented from just sliding through his life, and he is forced to begin dealing with matters of significance. (*Evan Almighty* is a terrific movie to watch to see a radical character transformation, by the way. Another is *Groundhog Day*.)

A knot often involves a fear. It might be the fear of being abandoned that has led the hero into unhealthy relationships, since that at least beats being alone. It could be the fear of not measuring up to a father's expectations, like Mozart in *Amadeus*. It might be the fear of being hurt or of losing loved ones, which could lead to withdrawing from everyone, including those who could be close friends or lovers (*Lars and the Real Girl*).

In *Sky High*, Will Stronghold (played by Michael Angarano) is afraid he will never develop superpowers. He's the son of the two greatest superheroes in the world, but on the eve of high school, he's still got zilch. He tries to hide his lack of powers from his parents by pretending to have super strength, but it's all a lie. He's afraid he'll be a colossal washout.

You can also build (um, tie?) great knots through bitterness, anger, self-deception, and a lack of forgiveness—to others or oneself.

What will be your hero's knot? In what way is she out of balance? It's important that you get a handle on this because you will be displaying it in the first fifty pages. So cast your mind across where you want to go with this story. What internal conflict do you want your hero to have, and what imbalance could you give her that would make that conflict most poignant?

❦ · INITIAL HERE, PLEASE · ❦

Your hero's initial condition is to his inner journey what establishing normal is to your external story. Just as you need to do some work early in the book to set up your character's life and the world of the novel before allowing the main story to intrude, so you need to establish the "before" condition of your hero in terms of his character arc.

Don't let me confuse you. In chapter six we talked about establishing your hero's normal. That was mainly about the observable externals in his life: his job, home, and friends. True, his personality and other aspects of his inner life were evident, and you will certainly be letting his inner journey knot show up in the same scenes in which you are establishing his external normal, but they bear discussion separately.

Indeed, every chapter of this book discusses something you'll be including in the first fifty pages of your novel, or we wouldn't be discussing it. I'm expending about two hundred pages to talk about what you must do in only fifty. So you will necessarily be doing several of these at the same time. You'll be establishing normal while revealing genre while planting information while setting the stakes and a dozen other things. For the sake of understanding, though, it works best to talk about them in isolation.

So I'll risk confusing you again by saying that you need to establish the normal of your hero's inner journey. Given that she has this particular imbalance or fear in her life, how is it affecting her as the novel begins? We need to see the unsteady equilibrium she's struck and is trying to live with. We need to see her in denial of what is true about herself.

We need to see him trying to get on *Battle of the Eighties Has-Beens*. We need to see her trying to be liked by the popular kids. We need to see him doing supermarket openings in the costume of a long-cancelled TV show. We need to see him being a villain though his heart isn't in it. We need to see her hiding out in her apartment while writing stories about fearless adventurers (*Nim's Island*). We need to see him so full of himself he wouldn't know a good friend if one bit him on the toe.

In a sense, the imbalance is a sickness. In theological terms, it's a sin. Medically, it's a cancer that is slowly killing your hero. It is, well, a *knot* that is keeping the rope from sliding through the eyelet so the mechanism can work properly.

Your hero is not healthy. There's an invisible tumor inside him that, if left untreated, will prove fatal. Your story acts as a pushy family doctor who is putting the pressure on him to start receiving treatment. The more the doc pushes, the more the hero resists.

Choose your poison. How can you show your hero somehow out of balance?

Her initial condition is determined by her knot. When you know how she is out of balance, you can figure out her initial condition fairly easily. So go back to your notes on your hero's knot or imbalance. With that firmly in mind, brainstorm twenty ways that such a sickness might manifest in her life.

Let's say your hero has one of the most awful knots of all: the fear that he is, in the final analysis, worthless. How would that affect his life? Depending on the seriousness of it, it could be anything from a compulsion to enter every contest he can find (in the hope that he will win and then, for that moment at least, not feel so useless) to becoming a mercenary and volunteering for the most dangerous, no-win missions possible (hoping to get killed by the enemy and thus allow the world to be rid of him).

You see, I hope, how your hero's knot will impact his behavior. It doesn't have to be all-consuming, but it has to be *some*-consuming, or he is not really out of balance.

What will it be for your hero? Once you know her illness, you can begin showing some of the symptoms. What might some of those be?

The initial condition in the inner journey is the starting point. It is the blah of his current situation. It's the unbalanced balance he's struck because it's the best he's figured out to do until something else can be found.

I find myself taking a perverse pleasure in painting my hero in his initial condition. It's dark fun to curse him with this condition and make its effects start coming out in his life. How absurd that he would be this way … but as long as he is, let's push things to an almost ridiculous extreme to show how sorely in need of a change he is. He doesn't see it, of course, or he's had plenty of practice justifying it, which amounts to the same thing. But I see it, and the reader sees it. And, boy, is he going to get it. Mwahahaa.

As you think about how you can reveal your hero's initial condition, keep in mind that you'll be doing it while you're also establishing normal, revealing the backdrop, and all the other things we've talked about so far and will talk about next. Synthesize your thinking and play with ideas for how you might do two or three of them in a single scene. We may talk about these elements individually, but you'll be presenting them together in the huge, glorious mishmash that is your first fifty pages.

❧ · THE INCITING EVENT · ❧

Frodo Baggins was the most upstanding of Hobbits. He had a bit of the Old Took in him, which caused him to spend inordinate amounts of time wandering the fringes of the Shire—and even going on *boats*. But on the whole he was a respectable lad who never had dreams of adventure or riches or anything else that might take him too far from his delightful Bag End at the end of Bagshot Row.

He was, in short, safe. Coddled, even. Sheltered from anything that might disrupt his dear Hobbiton, and unaware of danger or evil or, indeed, how his lifestyle was truly special and worth fighting to preserve. He might be utterly heroic in his heart, but he could not know it, for it had never been tested.

Talk about a person in need of an inciting event.

A baby bird might have perfect wings and the desire to soar, but his tendency will be to stay right where he is. His yearning to fly might cause him to sigh periodically and gaze across the meadow, but the nest is too safe, warm, and familiar to resist. Why would he ever leave?

Someone's got to come along and push him out of the nest. Nudge, nudge, shove, shove, and then … oopth. Bye-bye.

Aaaaagh!

What's happening to me? I'm falling! No, I'm too young to die! If only I had a way to—

Hey … whoa. What am I doing? Where did those things come from? I didn't know they could do that. I didn't know *I* could do that.

Whee! Look, Ma, look at me! Woohoo! I can *fly*!

All right, back to regular narrator voice now (though the excursion to fowl language was fun, ahem).

Your main character is sick. We've established that by examining his knot and his initial condition. Maybe he knows he's got a problem, or maybe he doesn't. In either case, he's not interested in changing. He may be in pain, but better the devil you know than the devil you don't. We all have inertia, the tendency to remain in whatever condition we're in. Your hero will have the inertia to stay how he is: either stuck in some bad situation or hurtling toward it at full speed.

No one, you and me included, changes until the pain of staying the same becomes greater than the pain of risking a change.

So something will have to come along to force him to change. The pain will have to be increased. Some shove is needed to knock him out of his current direction and send him screeching along a detour.

Dear old Frodo probably would've stayed in the Shire for the rest of his days if he'd been allowed to. He had wealth and status and a stout little gardener for a friend. But into his life came the Ring of Power, a talisman made of the evil that constituted the Dark Lord's very essence. The passing of the Ring into Frodo's possession was, to quote *The Lord of the Rings*, as the coming of doom.

Because the Dark Lord wanted it back, you see. Until he had it on his finger again, his power was incomplete. But if he could re-claim it, all of Middle-earth would fall under the cloud. And so he expends all his might in the effort to find it, and he sends forth all the beings that answer his call to find the one who has the Ring, cut it off his finger (hand included, if needs be), and bring it back to the Black Gate.

When Frodo gets the Ring, he realizes he can no longer stay in the Shire. All the happy expectations he had of living out his days as a simple hobbit gentleman are erased. Now, if he cares at all about his home and his people, he must take the Ring far away from them. At first, his mind is only on taking it from them to remove their danger, hoping to give it to someone else to take care of so he can quickly return to Bag End. But the story has other plans. The story is going to show him of what stuff this hobbit is made, and it will ask him to give everything in the effort.

The coming of the Ring was the inciting event in Frodo's life. It was the wrench thrown in the gears, the unlooked-for interruption that made him change his plans—and, ultimately, arrive at his own moment of truth.

What will it be for your hero? She is beset by a particular illness that has manifested itself in certain ways as the story begins. She might be feeling a little off, but she sees no need for drastic changes, and certainly not now. Maybe mañana.

What delightful catastrophe will you drop on her head?

Joe Kingman (Dwayne Johnson's character in *The Game Plan*) expected to keep living the high life of a star NFL quarterback and most eligible bachelor. But then ding-donging at the door comes a little girl, a daughter he never knew he had. Uh-oh, detour time. He doesn't realize it yet, but this pesky kid who is ruining his foot-loose lifestyle is going to cause him to find himself.

Will Stronghold doesn't know it, but the people he meets on his first day of superhero high school are going to become the triggers that release his own superpowers. Lightning McQueen (in Pixar's *Cars*) doesn't see it, but getting lost in the Podunk town of Radiator Springs is going to be the thing that causes him to mature from utter selfishness to a person (er, car) of worth. Lawrence doesn't know it, but getting sent into the Arabian Desert is going to be the very thing he needed to discover who he is.

Your hero doesn't see it yet, but X is going to be the very thing she needs to find herself. She's not even aware she's lost herself or has a problem at all, perhaps, but that doesn't mean it's not true.

So what wrecking ball are you going to slam into her life? What unlooked-for development are you going to drop onto her path?

There are only two prerequisites for a good inciting event. First, it must be perfectly chosen to spin her off in a direct tangent toward her moment of truth. If you want her to come to grips with her fear of displeasing her mother, the inciting event probably can't be that she gets the wrong order at Denny's. Whatever it is, it has to be well aimed. Second, it has to be strong—strong enough that she can't just ignore it and successfully go back to her life. Make it a big deal. Bring the pain.

You know your hero better than anyone else does. Pick an inciting event that has her name all over it.

❧ BEGIN THE TRANSFORMATION ❧

Perhaps the most gratifying thing about reading a novel is watching someone transform. When we see a person in an unbalanced position, we can relate to it. We all have areas where we're not entirely "fixed." We all have cognitive dissonance about something in our lives, simultaneously holding to opposing views. We all know what it's like to be torn or feeling like we have to behave in ways that aren't really us.

So we recognize that in characters in novels and movies. We secretly want to see what happens to them. We get a kind of voyeuristic pleasure—or perhaps an existential revelation—when we watch others try to navigate waters similar to the ones we find ourselves adrift in.

A character's transformation has well-known waypoints. Like a caterpillar becoming a butterfly, there are stages—egg, caterpillar, pupa, butterfly—that a character will go through on the way to his moment of truth and final state. When you know these stages, you can write them well. And when you write well the stages of a character's transformation, you will delight your reader.

The first fifty pages of your novel will show your hero in the earliest points along this journey: the knot, initial condition, and inciting event. They are crucial milestones without which you will have no satisfying inner journey. But if you do have them, you will have the makings of a novel that can be something special indeed.

What personal revelation do you want your hero to make in this story? When you know that, you can see the steps required for him to get there.

CHAPTER 9
HOW TO BEGIN

He who chooses the beginning of a road chooses the place it leads to. It is the means that determine the end. **—HARRY EMERSON FOSDICK**

EVERY CHAPTER IN THIS BOOK—AND THE BOOK itself—could be titled "How to Begin." Later, I'll talk about the very first line of your novel and then the first page, so maybe that chapter should be "How to Begin." But I've given the title to this chapter because we're going to talk about the structure of your opening. Architecturally speaking, this is how to begin.

How have you imagined your book beginning? Do you see it as an opening extravaganza that establishes your story world but not your main character? Are you thinking you'd start with your hero running for her life and throwing herself off a precipice and then slapping a "Three Weeks Earlier" on the page and spending the rest of the book catching up to that moment? (*Megamind* starts that way.) Had you envisioned an old character narrating a story that we then see as flashback (à la *Titanic*)?

There are as many ways of starting a novel as there are novels, of course, but they tend to fall into four main categories: prologue, hero action, *in media res*, and frame device. Let's look at these options. One of them is the right "How to Begin" for your book.

❦· PROLOGUE ·❦

A prologue is a scene or sequence that takes place outside of the main action of the book but that has direct bearing on the story. The etymology of *prologue* is "a speech beforehand" or "words that come before" from the Greek *prologos* ("before words").

Prologues can feature the hero, or they can feature other characters entirely. The prologue of *Mulan* introduces the villain character, Shan-Yu, as he and his army swarm over the Great Wall of China and begin their invasion. The prologue of *Indiana Jones and the Last Crusade* features the hero as a boy.

Prologues can be extremely useful little tools for the novelist or screenwriter. They can establish things we've talked about (the hero, "normal," tone, genre, backdrop, era, setting, engage your reader, etc.) and things we haven't covered yet (like villain, stakes, ticking time bomb), all in one brilliant scene that can be just about anything you want. Unlike every other scene in a novel, a prologue doesn't even have to advance the main story, because the main story hasn't started yet. It has bearing on the main story, of course, but is, in a sense, outside it. It's a freebie.

Despite its many splendors, the prologue has fallen out of favor in some fiction circles, mainly among a certain subset of agents and acquisitions editors. (Hopefully by the time you read this it will no longer be true, and you'll wonder what in the world Jeff is talking about.)

The thinking goes that prologues are bad. Either because "no one" reads them or because they have tended to be nothing but information dumps. The editors and agents who hold to this belief will go so far as to reject a book simply because the word "Prologue" appears at the top of page 1. I once saw an editor at a writers conference tear off an author's prologue and throw it on the floor, unread.

This is, as I hope seems obvious to you, ridiculous. Rejecting a book simply because of this word printed at the top of the page makes as much sense as rejecting it because the author is right-handed. (Lefties rule!)

Now, if the prologue is indeed nothing but an information dump (telling), then by all means it should be thrown out. But that's because telling is bad craftsmanship, not because it was called a prologue. Telling should be cut out of a novel just about anywhere it occurs, and especially in the first fifty pages. But it's not as if it would be perfectly fine to fill the opening pages of your novel with backstory just so long as you wrote "Chapter One" across the top instead of "Prologue."

So let's take the silliness off the table, all right? If you want to begin with a prologue, do so. Just make sure there is no telling in it. Readers do read prologues in fiction, so don't worry about that. Prologues can be helpful little guys for your novel. Put them back into the list of legitimate ways to begin your book.

(If you find out that an agent or editor you're about to show your manuscript to is a card-carrying anti-prologue advocate, delete *Prologue* from the top of page one and change it to *Chapter One*. Keep all the text the same, of course. Renumber the rest of your chapters, and you're golden. Seriously. Just … no telling.)

All right, with that out of the way we can get back to why prologues are good things.

You may not realize that some of your favorite movies actually begin with prologues, so let me go through a few.

Ice Age begins with a delightful prologue about Scrat (a prehistoric squirrel) chasing his acorn across a glacier and inadvertently setting off disaster. By the time he hits the ground far below and the main character is introduced, we know a lot about this story world and the tone this movie is going to have. We're well prepped for what is to come.

Ghostbusters starts with a creepy paranormal encounter in the New York Public Library. Our main characters haven't even come on yet, but we're being set up for what they'll be doing. As we have seen, *The Hunt for Red October* begins with Sean Connery riding in a Soviet missile sub on a cold Russian morning and *Enemy at the Gates* begins with Vassili needing to shoot his rifle at a wolf on another cold morning in Mother Russia. These prologues introduce us to a major character in the movie and set the stage for the story.

Dante's Peak begins with vulcanologist Dr. Harry Dalton (played by Pierce Brosnan) who, with his fiancée, has stayed too late to study a Colombian volcano. It erupts, killing Dalton's fiancée as they flee. The main story picks up four years later as this wounded hero is called in to study yet another simmering volcano.

Reign of Fire begins with our hero as a boy. Underground in a mine in England he stumbles upon the lair of a long-dormant dragon, who awakens and ushers in the Armageddon that, as an adult, he spends the rest of the movie trying to survive.

Both *Sky High* and *Nim's Island* begin with fanciful prologues that give a ton of backstory in an entertaining way. Disney's *Aladdin* begins with two prologues—one that introduces us to the story world and another that sets up the villain.

The prologue is your friend.

In a prologue you can knock out nearly half the things you must do in the first fifty pages of your novel. If that idea appeals to you, give another thought to using one.

Think of a prologue as a short story. Or, to use our cinema metaphor, as a short film. Make it a standalone narrative that would work as a complete little story unto itself. The opening sequence in

Indiana Jones and the Last Crusade is a great example. It's essentially a short film that could be entered into film festivals all by itself. It works as a self-contained piece of cinematic entertainment. It takes place independently of the main story but has bearing on it.

Not that a prologue must necessarily be short. They usually are, but there's nothing that says they can't be longer. In my fourth novel, *Operation: Firebrand*, I wrote a four-chapter sequence that functioned as a prologue. My hero began as a sniper for a Navy SEAL team deployed in Indonesia. Throughout the course of this extended prologue I had him go with his team to take out a target of opportunity, but the mission goes horribly wrong. The fallout over this, which took several pages to adequately deal with, set up what the hero would do in the main story, which begins some time after that mission.

Prologue doesn't mean "short scene," after all. It just means words before, as in words that come before the main action, words that have to come first to predispose the reader to encounter the primary story as he should. If you feel that a prologue would be a great way to start your book, go for it. And make it as long or as short as you need it to be to accomplish your objectives.

One of the great advantages to a prologue is that you can use it to engage your reader but you don't have to show your hero doing something active. As we have seen, if you begin with your protagonist onstage, you are forced to make her do something intrinsically interesting activity, or you won't engage your reader. But what if she's not doing anything interesting at the outset? What if she doesn't become a superhero until the mysterious meteorite falls from the sky and gives her powers (as in *Monsters vs. Aliens*)? Too bad. If you're starting with her onstage, you have to figure out something heroic and bigger than life for her to do, even without her powers.

That's a lot of burden to put on your opening. It might result in you artificially cramming your hero into activities he wouldn't really be undertaking at this point in the story. And starting a novel by already violating what is believable for your hero is a Bad Idea.

But if you use a prologue to perform the duty of engaging the reader, then the first time you bring your hero onstage, you can have him doing something perfectly typical for him, even if it's not fascinating in and of itself.

The first time we meet Dr. Spengler (Bill Murray's character in *Ghostbusters*), he's performing bad science and flirting with a girl. It's a great introduction to reveal his character, but it's not exactly epic action. No worries, though, because the story began with that haunting at the library. The viewer is hooked, which means the protagonist's first scene doesn't have to worry about doing that too.

Because we have seen Shan-Yu and his army swarming over the Great Wall of China, we are engaged in the story. We know bad guys are coming and a war is brewing. So when the filmmakers bring Mulan onstage, they don't have to force that scene to bear the burden of engaging the viewer. They don't have to contrive some action set piece to introduce Mulan the warrior girl. They can simply show her in her natural habitat. They can concentrate on depicting her normal and acquainting us with who she is as a character. That's the beauty of a prologue.

If you decide to write a prologue, be sure it's a good long scene. No half-page "prologues." You'd be hard-pressed to come up with a movie that begins with a ten-second scene, so don't give the equivalent of that in your novel. Don't give us one or more little scenes, because they feel like stutter-steps, halting lurches instead of a graceful dance run. When you start your book, well and truly *begin* it.

Start with a scene that lasts eight to twenty pages, which in a novel is about the scale of the opening scene in a movie.

Finally, remember that your prologue, should you choose to write one, needs to engage your reader. It may be doing other things, too, like introducing your hero or villain, but whatever else it does, because it occupies your opening pages it must therefore accomplish Job One of your first fifty pages, which is to hook your reader.

So what about it? If you've been thinking a prologue is right for your novel, I hope you have new encouragement to do so. If you weren't thinking of a prologue to begin your book, why not at least toy with the idea? Brainstorm six or eight short stories you could create that would be wonderful ways to launch your novel. It won't hurt to think about it, and you can always decide to go with your original thought. I find that considering options has a way of either giving me awesome new ideas or confirming that my first plan was best.

❧· HERO ACTION ·❧

A variant of the prologue is what I'm calling hero action. When a story opens with this kind of scene, it happens before the main action of the story (because you still have to establish normal before you violate normal) but it is action that shows the hero in his current situation, whereas a prologue might feature the hero many years before the main story begins.

The classic example, as I've mentioned, is the opening sequence in *Raiders of the Lost Ark*. Watch that sequence again and analyze how many things it accomplishes that we talk about in this book. Indy comes home from that trip and is almost immediately thrust into the main action of the story.

Every James Bond movie begins with 007 as a secret agent in his prime doing his thing to eliminate bad guys. He wins the day (usually) and then drops by MI6 to flirt with Miss Moneypenny and get his next mission.

Hero action openings are used to introduce the protagonist. If you've decided to engage your reader by showing the hero on-stage as the curtain rises, this is usually how you will want to begin your novel.

Note that hero action doesn't have to mean action action. Elle Woods (Reese Witherspoon's character in *Legally Blonde*) steps onstage full of the confidence that comes from being president of a popular sorority on a large university campus in southern California. She and all her sorority sisters are expecting her boyfriend, a future Harvard law student, to propose to her and sweep her away to the kind of life she's been working to achieve. Before the scene comes in which they're sitting across the restaurant table from each other and he drops the bomb, we have already seen our hero in action. We've gotten to know her as popular and girlie, but also as sharp as a tack, at least when it comes to fashion. It's a hero action beginning in which the action doesn't involve spies or cannibalistic tribesmen.

Nancy Drew begins with Nancy (played by Emma Roberts) doing—what else?—solving a crime. We see our hero in action just before the main story begins. We see her as not only a great sleuth but a mature young woman who talks law and psychology to crooks and then dangles from a building in a daring escape. It's a terrific hero action scene to introduce the main character and reveal a lot about her—and about the tone of the movie.

I, Robot opens with a scene in which our hero, Detective Spooner (played by Will Smith), assumes a robot has committed a crime and commences to chase the robot down on foot to try to arrest it. We see him show off his physical fitness, determination, and, unfortunately, his prejudice … because the robot isn't committing a crime at all. This hero action scene introduces a great deal of information about who this person is and what kind of world the story will take place in.

Gladiator begins with Maximus (Russell Crowe) leading his troops in a fantastic battle against a barbarian horde. We see him care for his men. We see his leadership. We see his personal heroism and prowess in battle. We're all but thumping our chests by the time the sequence is over. Now *that's* a good hero action opening.

Perhaps your novel would work best if it began with a hero action scene. When you craft a sequence that 1) reveals who the hero is at his core, 2) shows (or at least hints at) his knot, 3) introduces the story world, tone, genre, etc., and 4) engages the reader, you have a terrific opening for your novel.

Maybe you'd been thinking of beginning your book with a prologue that happens two hundred years before the main action begins. That might actually work, but give some thought to beginning with the hero onstage doing what he'll be called upon to do in the course of your novel.

Even if you do decide to begin with a prologue or some other mechanism for launching your novel, you can always use a hero action scene for the first time we see your protagonist onstage.

And remember to make it a good long scene. No halting steps as you begin your book.

❧· IN MEDIA RES ·❧

In media res is Latin for "in the middle of things." In storytelling, it refers to beginning not at the beginning but either in the middle or at the end.

Megamind begins with our protagonist falling from the sky. By means of voice-over narration, he informs us that he's about to show us how he came to be in this situation. Ninety percent of the rest of the movie shows the story of what led to him falling from the sky. We start near the end, then flash back to see what happened earlier. Near the end, we "catch up" to that moment, and when we see him falling from the sky, not only do we understand how it happened but we feel much differently about him than we did at the outset.

The Emperor's New Groove starts with our main character, Kuzco (voiced by David Spade) sitting alone in the rain and in the form of a llama. How he got into that fix is the subject of the rest of the movie.

An *in media res* opening can be a tremendously effective way to begin your novel. It all but guarantees that you're starting with action that will engage your reader (because who jumps ahead in a story to begin with something boring?). It gives your novel a running start and, if done well, raises in your reader all kinds of intrigue about what's happening and why. With an opening like this, you can so hook your reader that, like with a prologue, your first "normal" scene can actually be pretty mundane.

TV show writers love *in media res* beginnings, especially as a way to bring variety to how their episodes usually begin. A classic example is the *Star Trek: The Next Generation* episode called "Cause and Effect." The opening shot shows our beloved starship, the *Enterprise*, in dire peril. Before forty-five seconds have elapsed, Captain Picard has ordered all hands to abandon ship, and then the *Enterprise* explodes.

Wow. Talk about engaging the viewer. Try blowing up all your main characters and your iconic spaceship and see if you don't get the reader's attention.

However, there are pros and cons to beginning in the middle of things with a novel. I don't believe it's for everyone, and I certainly don't believe it's for every novel. It takes more mastery to do well than it might first appear.

I have seen far too many unpublished novels that begin with the hero running away from the creatures or the bad guys or whatever. Then we get a "Two Years Earlier" stamp at the top of the next chapter, and the book goes back to how it all began.

Sounds fine, right? Sounds like a good *in media res* beginning. But the problem was that I just didn't care. I had no previous connection with this character, and I didn't get one in this scene, so I didn't actually mind too much if the zombies got her.

To work, an *in media res* opening has to do what any other kind of novel opening has to do: It must engage the reader. There must be some kind of intrigue generated to connect the reader with what's going on, or else it's failed. And if your opening fails, the rest fails, too. After an *in media res* opening, the next scene is typically less action-oriented or intrinsically interesting. So you've got to be really engaging with your opening, or you'll have bigger problems on your hands.

In contrast to the types of beginnings we've looked at in this chapter already, an *in media res* opening usually works best if it's pretty short. A little confusion is good for the reader. It makes her lean forward to try to figure out what's going on. Too much confusion—as would happen with an extended opening in which characters are deep into relationships and plot-specific actions—is bad for the reader. Your story will appear to be random people running around doing random things for random reasons.

Inception, Memento, The Jerk, and *The Life of David Gale* are examples of movies that begin *in media res*. Some, like *Inception* and *Memento*, are largely concerned with the workings of the mind or memory. In cases like that, an *in media res* opening is often warranted. Other times, it's just plain fun.

There's something thrilling about catching up to that starting point. Such stories feel holistic and complete. Some of these stories end pretty much at that point when the circle is completed. Others catch up to that moment but then keep going. Those are my favorites. Everything before has felt a little predestined, since we know in the back of our minds that we're going to eventually return to that starting point. But when we pass that point and keep going, it feels fresh and freewheeling as if we're now performing without a net.

As Sarah Connor (Linda Hamilton's character in *Terminator 2*) says at the end, "The future, always so clear to me, had become like a black highway at night. We were in uncharted territory now ... making up history as we went along."

Let's think about your novel. Does it involve time travel or the mysteries of the brain? If so, an *in media res* opening might be just the ticket for you. Are you writing a series and this is book four? If so, it could be very cool to show your main character in some dangerous or unexpected situation, then make readers wait to find out how he got in that fix. Is your hero not especially heroic at the beginning and you want to start with action but not a prologue? Or are you just looking for a novel way to begin your book?

If one or more of those is true, you might look into beginning in the middle of things. Keep in mind that these are harder to pull off than pretty much any other kind of opening structure. Indeed, I don't think I've ever recommended for publication a novel that began *in media res*. Not because I'm against that style, but because the authors attempting it didn't do it well.

It's almost always better to go with a straight chronological arrangement for your novel. That applies to the first fifty pages and all the pages that come after. You already know how I feel about flashbacks, so you understand why I say that an entire book done as a flashback is going to run the risk of boring the reader. If you have no compelling reason to try this kind of opening, I recommend you avoid it.

But if you do have a good reason, or you just want to attempt it, go for it. You can only strengthen your book by playing with alternate ideas.

❧ THE FRAME DEVICE ❧

The final "How to Begin" mechanism we'll look at is the frame device. This is when you begin and end your novel in some time and place other than that in which the main story takes place.

Titanic is a good example of a frame story. We see our modern-day *Titanic* researchers and we meet an old woman named Rose who claims to know about the diamond the researchers are hoping to find. Rose travels to the researchers' ship and proceeds to tell her tale. As she speaks, we are sent back in time with her words, and we see the story play out as if it were happening "live."

Several times through the movie we come back to modern day, mainly to ground us in that reality and to allow for time to be skipped over in the past story. And after we've heard the whole saga, we come back to the researchers' ship and see how Rose's own story ends.

Another example of a frame device structure is *The Notebook*. An old man tells an old woman a story of two young lovers, and we go back in time to watch it all unfold. Throughout the movie we come back to the older couple, but then it's back to the past for more flashback.

A frame story could work for your novel. These are the narrated, "as told to" kind of stories in which someone is recapping something that came before. In that sense, it's very similar to an *in media res* opening, except a frame story is almost always done long after the events, not in the middle of them.

One of the downsides of a frame device story is that you lose a certain amount of tension. If you show your hero as an old man, every scene in the past when you put him in danger becomes humdrum—because we know he lives. You undercut your suspense.

However, so long as you're keeping that in mind, it's possible to sidestep that issue. Just be ambiguous about who is telling the story. We think it's the hero, but it could be his brother, his rival, or his son. And the old woman with him—she could be the girl from the story, but she could also be someone else.

Another trick to making frame device stories work is to have something happening in the modern story as well as the story in the past. If we just have a person sitting in an easy chair doing her once-upon-a-time spiel, it will be harder to keep the reader engaged in those sections. But if you have suspense, action, and relationships happening in both stories, it's possible to make both stories interesting.

Marduk's Tablet by T.L. Higley is a novel about a modern-day philologist who goes to an archaeological dig to decipher the symbols on an ancient clay tablet. There is intrigue and mayhem in this story, as someone wants to keep the tablet secret. But whenever the hero touches the tablet, she is sent back in time and walks around in the mind and body of a Babylonian priestess. There is danger and suspense and relationship development in that story, as well. Throughout the novel, we go back and forth between the two. And since both stories are interesting in and of themselves, the frame device works.

As I said above, I am of the opinion that stories are almost always better executed when laid out in a straight chronological order. A frame device story is essentially a very long flashback, with all the pitfalls and risks of any flashback. If you do a good job of getting your reader engaged with your story, what's going to happen to that interest when you stop the main story to go tell some other story? When you ask your reader to suspend caring about one group of characters and start all over again with a new set, you risk having him say, "Um, no thanks. Wonder what's on television."

So why would someone consider a frame device structure for a novel? Several reasons. One, a frame story might be best if you feel it might be too hard for the reader to connect with your hero and her situation. Take *Marduk's Tablet*, for instance. If the back cover copy for that book informed the potential reader that it was all about the adventures of an ancient Babylonian priest-ess, it would've been a hard sell. But to be able to say that it was about an eager young American woman trying to make sense of a relic while running for her life in the Middle East ... ah, now that'll sell.

So if your book is about something so far removed from read-ers or what they think they'd like to read about, a frame device might be the way to bridge that gap.

Second, you might consider a frame story if you want to tell two stories in two eras. *Julie & Julia* is a great example of this kind of story. We're fascinated by Julia Child's story in the past, but the thing that keeps us hooked is Julie Powell's story in the present. *Sophie's Choice* is another example of the frame device done very effectively. Maybe you've got a dual-era story like these. If so, con-sider a frame device.

Third, a frame story might work for you if you want to keep your reader in suspense about how the story turns out. Of course you want to generate suspense about your ending no matter what kind of opening you use. But the frame device allows you to lead and mislead your reader about who has lived, who has died, and who has hooked up with whom. You can show characters in the scenes from the modern story and lead us to believe that it might be X or it might be Y. That can be wicked fun.

Finally, you might consider a frame device if you're writing a time travel story. *Back to the Future* begins and ends in 1985, but in the middle we're in 1955. And the 1985 we come back to is far different from the one we left. That's a cool use of the frame story. Any novel in which you're playing around with time or memory is a good candidate for the frame device.

❧· REMEMBER: ENGAGE THE READER ·❧

How to begin your novel? I hope this chapter has caused you to consider a different opening than you'd first assumed you'd go with.

Most novels start with either a prologue or the hero action opening. Those would be the most typical, comprising probably 85 percent of fiction being written and published today. But that doesn't mean it has to be how you start your book.

You can also create your own sort of hybrid. Why not do a frame story in which the modern-day storyline begins *in media res*? Why not have a prologue that establishes the villain, but then later we see that it was really a frame device and our hero turns into that villain? Fun, fun.

What opening does the movie *The Bourne Identity* use? It starts with a mystery man floating unconscious in the Mediterranean Sea in a black ops outfit and some kind of locator beacon. Fishermen pull him out of the drink and find he's been shot several times. They nurse him back to health, but when he comes to, he doesn't remember who he is. The rest of the movie involves him trying to regain his memory—and then, when he does remember, he wants out of the life that had gotten him shot.

It's not a prologue opening, exactly, because we don't see anything before the main story begins. Nor is it a hero action beginning, because floating unconscious isn't anyone's definition of action. And it certainly doesn't introduce us to the hero—because even he doesn't know who he is. We discover his personality as he does … along the way. It could be an *in media res* start because obviously he's in the middle of something big. But we don't then jump back to earlier in his story. Except, sort of. And it isn't a frame story, precisely, though everything he does in the present is designed to figure out what happened in the past.

Actually, it isn't important to identify what kind of opening it has. It's some kind of variant on two or more kinds. What *is* important to notice is that it performed Job One: It engaged the audience. In the final analysis, that's the primary question you should be asking when you think about how to do your opening, no matter which structure you use to begin: Will this engage my reader?

Hopefully this discussion has given you some good ideas for beginnings to investigate, but if what you've come up with doesn't fit any of these categories but does engage the reader and get her pointed in the right direction for your book, go for it.

CHAPTER 10
ANOTHER FINE MESS

A hard beginning maketh a good ending. –JOHN HEYWOOD

HAVE YOU EVER READ A NOVEL OR WATCHED A MOVIE in which nothing happens? Oh, people talk and events occur, but in terms of what makes for a good story, nothing really happens.

I have. I've seen so many (unpublished) fiction manuscripts that are filled with character interactions, interesting vignettes, delightful locations, intriguing personalities, and, often, tons of backstory, but that never seem to get off the couch and go do something, literarily speaking.

This kind of story is usually written by the character-first novelist, the author who gets brilliant ideas for wonderful characters but whose ideas for plot pale in comparison. I don't mean to pick on writers like that. Their character and dialogue work is usually ten times better than whatever I come up with naturally. It's just how they're made that they can think of seventeen incredible characters before one decent plot point. The trick is to figure out how to keep the one and add the other. (If this is you, my e-book called *How to Find Your Story* will help you.)

Without an obstacle to try to overcome, even the best-written character has no *raison d'être*. At its most fundamental level, fiction is about someone who wants something—and the thing that would keep him from getting it.

Stories that lack an obstacle tend to meander along feeling aimless—not only to readers but to the author. It's no wonder, because if you don't know what destination you were trying to reach, how will you know if you've gotten there?

What your story needs, and what you must introduce in the first fifty pages, is what (or who) is standing in the way of what your character wants.

I'm talking about villain/antagonist, and I'm also talking about stakes, conflict, and suspense.

For your story to be wonderful, you have to get your hero into another fine mess.

❧· VILLAIN ·❧

For every Luke Skywalker there must be a Darth Vader. For every Wyatt Earp there must be a Billy Clanton. And for every Ripley there must be an alien queen. In hero's journey terminology, this is the shadow. The hero's evil opposite.

Your hero is only as strong as the antagonist against which she is pitted. If Ellen Ripley (Sigourney Weaver's character in *Aliens*) saved a little girl from, say, a trio of angry carpenter ants, she wouldn't be very heroic. But have her square off against an armored alien the size of a tractor, with acid for blood and teeth that extend to rip out your throat, and now you've got the makings of a heroic story.

Standing between your hero and his objective is the villain. That doesn't mean it has to be a guy with a chainsaw. It could be a boss or a rival in love. It doesn't even have to be a person. It could be an illness, a corporation, a mountain, a disability, or even time itself. So long as you've got some obstacle that is positioned so as to prevent your protagonist from achieving his goal, you've got what's required.

Most novels are best served by having an identifiable bad guy. You need someone to personify the challenge to the hero's desire. It's all well and good to have your hero going up against "the English," but how do you illustrate that? Just large armies? A big castle? From a structural perspective, you need a King Edward I for your William Wallace to rail against. When Edward is defeated (or when Edward is victorious), you'll know the story is over.

You can have Harry Potter stand up against Evil, but how? Without "He Who Will Not Be Named," ol' Harry wouldn't have anything to square off against. It would be specific Good against generic Evil, and it wouldn't work as a story. You need someone at whom to throw your darts.

Even if your antagonist is a system, a mode of thinking, or a bureaucracy, you need someone to symbolize it. George "Bright Eyes" Taylor (Charlton Heston's character in *Planet of the Apes*) was really up against the entire simian civilization. But that wouldn't have been very cinematic. How do you know if you're making any headway against a civilization? Ah, but if you have a Dr. Zaius to represent that civilization, you can know where you stand. If Zaius is triumphing, simian culture is triumphing. But if Taylor were able to get the edge on Zaius, it would represent progress gained against the civilization.

Both Eli (Denzel Washington's character) in *The Book of Eli* and the Postman (Kevin Costner's character) in *The Postman* are going up against anarchy in a postapocalyptic America. They can have battles against various groups, but you need a personified *boss* to know when the war is won. And so we have Carnegie (Gary Oldman) and General Bethlehem (Will Patton).

Robert Neville (Will Smith's character in *I Am Legend*) is fighting a horde of mutants swarming across Manhattan. But that's too vague an antagonist, so the screenwriters created the Alpha Male character to be the king of the mutants and thus a much more useful villain.

I suspect you've given thought to who the villain is going to be for your book. Whether you have or you haven't, think about it right now. Maybe you've got a clear villain in mind. If so, great. We'll talk in a minute about what characteristics this person should have. But if your hero's goals are obstructed by something more abstract, consider how you might coalesce that villainy into a character you might invent.

Most of the time, it's best to have a personified villain. It's just so much more satisfying to allow your hero to finally face off against his nemesis, to let the accused stand before his accuser, than to have him spitting into the wind.

But sometimes the story you're telling simply can't have an embodied villain. Man vs. man stories almost always will, but there are other categories. There is also man vs. nature, man vs. self, man vs. technology, man vs. society, and man vs. the supernatural or Fate. If the thing standing in the way of your hero is an asteroid hurtling toward Earth, as in *Armageddon*, you're not going to have someone personify the asteroid. If your antagonist is Fate, as in *Groundhog Day*, there will probably be no Mr. Fate to go toe-to-toe with. If your villain is a string of deadly tornados or a perfect storm, you don't need it to be incarnated into a human.

Sometimes you actually can generate a personified enemy from one of those categories. Man vs. technology can pit a hero against a Terminator or a mainframe computer (as in *I, Robot*). Man vs. nature can be illustrated as a hero against a great white shark. Man vs. self can be externalized as a hero against a character who is her shadow self, as Belloq says to Indiana Jones, "I am but a shadowy reflection of you. It would take only a nudge to make you like me. To push you out of the light."

Give some thought to creating a specific instance of your general villainous force. It may be the very thing your book was lacking to give it the conflict it needed. But don't force it. A more abstract villain may be better. Sometimes it really is Joe vs. the volcano.

CHARACTERISTICS OF A GOOD VILLAIN

To function as the blocking force for your hero, an antagonist has to possess certain qualities. These are things you'll be introducing in your first fifty pages.

For one thing, the villain has to oppose your hero. Sounds obvious, I know, but it bears mentioning. If your hero is trying to get accepted into UCLA film school, and your villain is an evil biologist poisoning all the frogs in South Africa, that may not be the best plan. Be sure your villain will directly block your hero's path.

That doesn't mean the connection has to be immediately evident. Perhaps the frog guy might actually be a good villain … if the hero's chances of getting into film school hang on his ability to complete a documentary about what's killing the frogs of South Africa. Sooner or later, though, the antagonist has to stand opposed to the hero, or he's someone else's villain.

Second, the villain has to be larger than life—powerful. This person has to represent a palpable threat to what the hero wants, or she is no villain. Pansy the Doe-Eyed Gardener is hardly going to create the legend of Thorak the Mighty, you know? The larger the villain looms, the more impressive is the hero's feat if he defeats him. Indeed, anyone who would even dare oppose an antagonist like Sauron (*The Lord of the Rings*), Voldemort (the *Harry Potter* movies), or the alien queen (*Aliens*) deserves credit just for starting out.

Is your villain powerful enough? Will defeating her make your protagonist look heroic? Even if you feel sure the answer is yes, go ahead and add a couple layers of villainy to her. If she's already dastardly, give her a Ring of Invulnerability and a Wand of Unmaking to boot. You need a villain of heroic proportions to create a hero of epic proportions.

One thing your villain does *not* have to be is mean. He doesn't have to act villainous. He doesn't even have to have the intent to thwart the hero. A mountain is a mountain, not an actively evil miscreant (in most stories, anyway). It might just be a mountain, and the storm might just be a storm. It's opposing the hero, but it doesn't have ill intent.

Even human villains don't have to be sinister mustache-twirlers. Dolores Umbridge (*Harry Potter and the Order of the Phoenix*) would never consider herself a villain. Nor would Clyde Shelton (Gerard Butler's character in *Law Abiding Citizen*). Other people certainly do, but that's not how their thinking goes. Same with any of "the other guys" in a war story or in a novel about sports. The members of the other side oppose the hero, but don't necessarily have to be wicked. In their minds, they are simply doing what must be done. If others oppose them and must be dealt with, so be it, but that doesn't make them bad.

Your villain doesn't have to be evil at all. Some stories, like *Legend* or *The Passion of the Christ*, demand it, but most do not. I think the creepiest heroes are the ones who are gray, especially if the hero (and the reader) can begin to sort of understand where the antagonist is coming from. She may not agree with what he's doing, but she can at least see why he's doing it. It's easy to write a pure black villain. But that makes it both a cliché and lazy writing. It's much harder, and therefore much more interesting for the reader, to paint your villain not with blacks and whites but in sixty-four-tone grayscale.

Make sure your villain blocks your hero's access to her goal, and make sure he is powerful. But think about leaving the black hat on the hat stand.

THE NO-VILLAIN STORY

Some stories have no villain. *Forrest Gump*, *Mary Poppins*, and *Being There* come to mind. These stories replace the antagonist with a sense of wonder and discovery. They are also usually from the special category of story in which the main character does not have an inner journey.

Now, that's not to say that a story with no character arc for the hero can't have a villain. WALL-E is pitted against AUTO, the ship's central computer, and any story of the life of Jesus will have Satan in it, though those are both stories in which the main character doesn't change.

If you're writing, for example, women's fiction about the lives and trials of four good friends in a coastal town in Maine, you probably won't have a bad guy. That's okay. No need to add a serial killer. Let it be what it is.

However, if you find yourself writing a story that feels like it should have no villain, think about it long and hard before you let yourself go there. It's much harder to write a novel in which the hero has no external enemy against which to strive. But certain stories will allow for it. If you're sure your book has all the conflict it needs without a villain, go for it.

INTRODUCING YOUR VILLAIN

If your novel has a villain, and most novels will, you'll need to bring her on in the first fifty pages.

How you introduce your antagonist needs every bit as much thought as how you bring your hero onstage the first time. Besides the protagonist, the villain is the most powerful character in the book. You could even argue that he's the *most* powerful character in the book, as he is probably the one making things happen. So his debut in your book needs to be done with intention. Besides, it's great fun to write villains.

If your book will allow it, I recommend you craft a scene for the villain that is, like your hero's introductory scene, essentially a short story, a standalone segment that shows us who he is and what he's like.

The first time we meet Yzma, the villain in *The Emperor's New Groove*, she's sitting in the Emperor's throne trying to run the country. Shortly after that we see her in her lair planning to poison the Emperor. When we meet the shark in *Jaws*, it attacks and devours a lone swimmer. Our initial glimpse of Darkness (Tim Curry's character in *Legend*) is of him on his throne plotting the overthrow of Light. Our first impression of Cal in *Titanic* is that he's an arrogant control freak.

Perhaps your story will allow you to bring the villain on later in the book, perhaps even beyond the first fifty pages. The alien in the original *Alien* movie doesn't appear until the very end of Act 1 (we'll discuss three-act structure in chapter eleven), and even then we don't see him until Act 2. HAL 9000 (in *2001: A Space Odyssey*) doesn't appear *as a villain* until after the midway point.

And sometimes you want to hide your villain's identity from the reader, as with a murder mystery. In these cases, the antagonist will be onstage for the reader to see, but she won't know which one of the characters parading before her eyes is the one who "dunnit."

We've already talked about the prologue as a way to begin your novel. I bring it up here because a prologue is often a terrific way to accomplish a number of things, including introducing your villain.

Before we ever meet Luke Skywalker, we've gotten a stunning introduction to Darth Vader. The opening scene of *Mulan* is a prologue about Shan-Yu bringing his army to destroy Mulan's world. *Stargate* begins with a scene in which the alien race abducts a primitive human for some obscure purpose. *Star Trek* (2009) starts with the introduction of Nero and the awesome firepower of his ship from the future.

Beginning your book with a scene introducing the villain is a good way to not only establish the antagonist and show the challenge the hero is going to be up against, but also to do some things we haven't talked about yet: set the stakes, show the OR-ELSE factor, begin the conflict, initiate the suspense, and set the ticking time bomb to ticking.

Further, a prologue introducing your villain removes from the scene in which you're going to introduce your hero the burden of also having to be independently suspenseful. Because the villainous prologue has engaged readers with suspense and pending danger, the hero's walk-on scene can catch her doing anything she would be doing, even if it's feeding chickens at the family farm or looking for a droid that also speaks Bocce (*Star Wars*).

Whether you introduce your villain on the opening pages of your novel or at some later point, do so in a way that characterizes her as powerful and sets us up properly for how to interpret her later when she brings the conflict against the hero. Your antagonist is a large part of getting your hero into another fine mess.

❧ CREATING SUSPENSE ❧

After successfully engaging the reader, which is Job One, it's tempting to say that Job Two is to create suspense. When your reader is engaged with your hero and your story world, you can coast along a bit before that begins to diminish (not that you would intentionally do so). But before too long you're going to need to continue reeling in the reader. He won't stay with you for the whole book if he gets bored soon after the opening.

Suspense means different things for different novelists—and different genres. If you're writing in the suspense/thriller genre, you'd better have a rollercoaster going pretty much from page 1. But if you're writing a romance, the suspense is more along the lines of whether or not the hero and heroine will get together finally or if they will miss each other and be miserable for the rest of their lives. It's the *will she or won't she* variety. Suspense might be in finding out if the hero will achieve his dream.

But the point is that there better be some kind of suspense in your novel. We talked earlier about the story question—whether or not the hero will achieve her goal—and that language can be used here as well. Let's call it the reader question. The reader must be asking, "How will this book turn out?," a question preferably followed by, "I have to find out, and I can't go to bed until I do!"

Some suspense will be created simply by engaging the reader with the main character. We want to see if he reaches his objective. Another surge of suspense will be generated when you introduce the villain, the equal and opposite force that's going to cause fits for your hero. Just having a person in there who stands to hurt our hero in some way will raise our excruciatingly wonderful anxiety. And excruciatingly wonderful anxiety would be a very nice definition for suspense. We can't stand it, but we love it.

Let's look at some other tools for raising suspense in the first fifty pages of your novel.

STAKES AND THE OR-ELSE FACTOR

If I told you I was going to give you a million dollars, you'd probably be thrilled. If I told you I would give you a million dollars if you could get to Clipperton Island (a tiny atoll eight hundred miles southwest of Acapulco) by noon tomorrow, you'd start feeling something else.

That something else—an almost frustrated kind of urgency tinged with the possibility of a great payoff—is what you want your reader feeling as she reads your novel.

There's a very simple formula for creating stakes (and thus suspense) in your novel: Show your reader something she wants, and then threaten it.

Show her a man longing to be reunited with his son. Show the son wanting to be back with his daddy. Then have someone abduct the boy and smuggle him to another country. Aaagh! How will that man find his little boy? Show me now!

Show a woman locked into an engagement with an awful man. Show a wonderful man she really loves and who loves her back. Then bring tremendous forces onto the woman to make her get married to the first guy no matter what. No! It can't be! She has to get with the good man.

Build in us affection for a ragtag group of freedom fighters who only want to live free of tyranny. Then show the evil Empire arriving with their Death Star to destroy the rebels' hidden fortress.

You see how it goes. Make us care about something, then put that something in danger. As the examples show, the danger doesn't have to be to life and limb. The prospect of the hero not getting what she dreams of, that we've come to dream of for her, is terrible enough.

What are the stakes in your novel? What does the protagonist long for, and how can you make it look like he won't get it? More importantly, what is the precious thing the *reader* longs for, and how will you threaten it?

In *Dante's Peak*, the stakes are that our hero and the woman and child he's come to love may not escape a volcano before it erupts and kills them all ... as another volcano killed the hero's fiancée years before.

In *Music and Lyrics,* the stakes are that the hero will take glory for himself alone instead of sharing it with his co-writer, and thus lose her love and the relationship they had been building together.

In *In the Line of Fire*, the stakes are that our hero, a Secret Service agent, may not put the puzzle together in time to save the president from an assassination attempt—as he failed to do for John F. Kennedy years before.

Another way of talking about stakes is in terms of the OR-ELSE factor. The hero will achieve her objective ... or else. But or else what? What bad thing will happen if she fails? If the protagonist and his crew don't figure out a way to deflect an incoming asteroid, the OR-ELSE is that Earth will be destroyed. If our FBI agent undercover in the beauty pageant doesn't find out who the killer is in time, the OR-ELSE is that someone will be brutally murdered. The bus can't drop below fifty miles per hour, or else the bomb will detonate.

You will establish the stakes, your OR-ELSE factor, in the first fifty pages of your novel. That doesn't mean we will know all about it in those pages. By the time we reach page 51 we may not know the exact bad thing that might happen, but we will have begun growing very attached to something or someone in the story, which is the first half of the formula: Show your reader something she wants, and then threaten it.

If you can lay out the stakes in those opening pages, by all means do so. It will give us longer to baste in that delicious angst. We'll talk more about this when we look at the ticking time bomb. For now, just file it away that the more pages the reader is aware of the stakes, the more she'll love to hate you for it.

It probably won't be until later in the novel that the precise form of that threat to what the reader wants becomes evident. He may know the what and the why, but the exact *how* will have to wait. We know the Empire wants to destroy the Rebel Alliance, but until the very end of Act 2 we don't know how they're going to try to do it. That's as it should be. But you can't wait so late to start building our connection with the thing we want—or to start laying the groundwork for how it could be taken away. Those things must be done in the first fifty pages.

THE TICKING TIME BOMB

From a fiction writer's point of view, the great thing about a countdown of any kind is that it increases suspense with every tick of the clock. The doom is hastening toward a conclusion—a negative conclusion, if the hero doesn't hurry up—and every moment we tarry is another moment lost to avoid that doom.

Your team is behind, and there are only twenty-five seconds left on the clock. Ack! Can they pull out a miracle? In five hours the last ferry leaves, and if she can't get him on that ferry with her, their future together will be lost. His baby has only six months to live if he can't find a cure. The race is tomorrow and their car is in pieces all over the garage.

Deadlines are wonderful things in fiction. (Well, they are for your characters. When you're *writing* under a deadline, that's not always so grand. But I digress.) In fiction, a ticking time bomb is a cut-off moment after which nothing more can be done to avert disaster. Accomplish your goal by then, or you've lost.

In *Mulan*, the ticking time bomb is established from the very beginning: An enemy army is coming and intends to destroy the Han Dynasty. It's crossed the only major line of defense, the Great Wall of China, and is bearing down on the simple villages of the people. Pretty early in *WarGames* we see that the WOPR computer is going to try to win a simulated game—by using very real global thermonuclear weaponry—in just over twenty-four hours. Possibly the best example is *Armageddon*, in which we learn early in the movie that an asteroid is on a collision course with Earth. Our heroes have to deflect or destroy it somehow, or it's the end of the human race.

Think about your novel. Can you plant a time bomb in it and start it counting down? It can be something large that you establish in a prologue or at some other spot in the first fifty pages, or it can be something that doesn't get going until near the end.

National Treasure 2 is an example of the latter kind. The time bomb is that the golden chamber is going to fill with water and kill everyone—unless our heroes can somehow get out in time. The water level is rising. There's not much time left. With every second that passes, the water goes up another inch. Soon there will be no chance for escape.

What can you do, on either a grand or a small scale, to use this dynamic in your novel? I can think of no better means of naturally increasing the tension in fiction. It's great because even when the writer isn't paying attention to it, the reader is still feeling it. The reader worries about its inevitable approach at all times. It's always in the background increasing that excellent suspense.

It's worth noting that the hero doesn't need to know the doom is coming. The main characters may be oblivious to the peril that is speeding toward them. It's enough that the reader knows. And sometimes that's a more excruciating kind of bliss. Maybe that's why people love to shout "Don't go in there!" to the characters on-screen in horror movies. We know what's about to happen, even if they don't.

As you think about creating suspense, do you see how a prologue could accomplish this for your story as well? No, not every novel should begin with a prologue, and not every prologue should introduce the villain, the stakes, and the ticking time bomb. But lots of them would be better if they began this way. Maybe yours is one of them.

Nor do you have to have a ticking time bomb in your story at all. You might be fine without it. But if Job Two is to keep your reader embroiled in suspense, why wouldn't you want to use a natural tension-generating device to help you accomplish that task? Give it some hard thought.

SHORTER PARAGRAPHS

One more tip about increasing suspense. This one's for free. Whether in your first fifty pages or anywhere else in your novel, when you want to subtly increase reader tension, use shorter paragraphs.

When I write, I tend to use fairly short paragraphs anyway, as I believe long paragraphs strain the eye and say to the reader, "I'm a boring book; don't read me!" (Indeed, I don't let my authors have paragraphs longer than seven lines in their fiction.) But when I want to up the tension, I use paragraphs that are even shorter still.

Shorter paragraphs read faster, which causes the eye to more quickly consume a page. This is a sneaky little physiological trick you can use to actually raise the reader's heart rate. The eye races across the page. The hands turn the pages more quickly. The pace is subtly sped up, and the result is a feeling of breathlessly sprinting to find out what happens. It's like faster intercutting in a movie.

Try it. Use longer paragraphs to simulate a slower pace. Then when you're ready to increase the tempo, start shaving the paragraphs down.

WHY YOUR HERO NEEDS OBSTACLES

Your goal is to drop your protagonist into another fine mess. There's a villain out there standing directly on the path to her goal. The villain is formidable. No one has defeated him—and no one who has tried has ever returned. To make it worse, if the hero can't get past the villain, her love will get on the train and go away forever, thinking she hadn't cared enough to come try to get him to stay. And to make it worse yet, that train is leaving in twelve minutes.

We knew your hero was likable and capable, but can she overcome this? Surely not. But she has to … she just *has* to. Off she runs, charging like Don Quixote at a windmill.

And we are right with her. Go, baby, go.

A hero without an obstacle, and without consequences if he should fail to overcome that obstacle, is a hero your reader may not care about. A strong villain, high stakes, and a relentless countdown will ratchet up the tension and make readers pull for your hero mightily.

Much of this can and should be accomplished in the first fifty pages.

CHAPTER 11

A ONE-ACT PLAY

Before beginning, prepare carefully. —CICERO

THERE IS WISDOM IN CONTEMPLATING THE STRUCTURE of something you are planning to build. You might feel an eagerness to lay the cornerstone and get busy actually *doing*, but large projects merit a good amount of *thinking* first.

Writing a novel is a large project. And while there is great benefit to sitting down and writing right when inspiration strikes, most often a novel written completely by the seat of your pants ends up a sprawling mess that neither you nor your reader can navigate. The solution isn't to discourage those times when the muse moves you, but to channel them along paths already charted out.

In this chapter we're going to look at three-act structure. Don't be alarmed, though. I have no intention of crimping your bouts of passionate writing. Nor will a discussion of structure result in a formulaic novel. A three-act structure is simply a way to be sure your novel is satisfying to the reader and includes everything you want the book to achieve.

In your first fifty pages you will be creating the foundation—laying the cornerstone—for the rest of your book. Your Act 1 may extend beyond the first fifty pages of the novel, or you may be on to Act 2 before those pages are up. Either way, no craft book on a novel's opening pages would be complete without a discussion of what needs to happen in Act 1.

❧• WHY STUDY THREE-ACT STRUCTURE? •❧

Three-act structure is a way of organizing a work of fiction. The "act" terminology betrays its origin as an idea developed in the realm of theater. Greek theater, to be precise. It is a storytelling framework that ensures you have included all the necessary pieces for a complete narrative construct.

I think all novelists can benefit from studying three-act structure. The plot-first novelists among us may feel they don't need any help with such things. I would counter that something you do by instinct may be something you haven't thought much about, and a modicum of thought devoted to it might just add skill to talent, and thus result in an overall enhancement of final effect.

But it is the character-first novelist who stands to gain the most from an examination of three-act structure. Character-firsters, as we have seen, create remarkably realistic characters but sometimes have no idea how to craft a satisfying plot. If I see a 200,000 word manuscript, my first guess is that it was written by a character-first novelist who simply had no way of knowing when she had reached the end—much less where any of the waypoints were along the way.

If you feel your stories tend to meander, or if you feel adrift when it comes to creating a solid plot, or if people try to "help" you find your story or complain that the book never seemed to go anywhere, this is a key chapter for you.

❧• THREE-ACT STRUCTURE—AN OVERVIEW •❧

You may have heard three-act structure explained as "beginning, middle, and end." That's a rough approximation, but it's imprecise and misleading, not to mention boring. If I had to use three words to describe the acts, I'd instead say, "Introductions, Heart, and Leap."

I like to explain three-act structure out of order, so prepare for a little mind-bending. I talk about Act 2 first. I do this because, when you understand Act 2, Acts 1 and 3 are easy to grasp.

Act 2 is the heart and soul of your novel. It is the reason you wanted to write this book. It is the time when you're doing the main thing you wanted to do.

Enemy at the Gates is a marvelous duel between two master snipers during the Battle of Stalingrad in World War II. Vassili Zaitsev (Jude Law's Russian sniper character) and Major König (Ed Harris's German sniper character) maneuver and plan and try to out-think their opponent. During this time we see the development of relationships, learn more about the characters, and see the conditions of the war and both armies. But it is the deadly mind vs. mind chess match between these two men that is the heart of this excellent film. In a way, the struggle between Vassili and König becomes symbolic not only of the Battle of Stalingrad but also of the entire war between Russia and Germany.

But consider: What if the filmmakers had started the movie with this duel? If they simply began the film by showing the center hour-plus of the film, the audience would be both confused and dispassionate. Oh, some guys are trying to shoot each other. Yawn.

Act 2 is the heart, but it isn't all you need. You also need some setup so you can understand and care about the people doing things onstage. Act 1 is the preparation you have to do so Act 2 can begin.

Nor could this duel, wonderful as it is, last forever. At some point, it must be concluded. One of these two men will have to win, and chances are that at least one of them will die. Act 2 is great fun, but again, it's not all you need. Act 3 is how you take the core of the story and bring it to a satisfying conclusion.

The heart of *WALL-E* is WALL-E's effort to win EVE's love. Sure, there are lots of goings-on during this time, as everyone tries to prevent or enable the spaceship's return to Earth. But as far as our little robotic hero is concerned, it's only about protecting and being near his beloved EVE. That's the fun middle section of the movie. The heart of the story, if you will.

But you see, I think, that they couldn't have started with WALL-E already aboard the *Axiom* chasing this other random robot for unknown reasons. We wouldn't know what was going on. Some groundwork had to be laid before that fun could begin. That's what Act 1 did.

Act 3 is how his quest to achieve EVE's love (oh, and save the human race) turns out. The merry-go-round might be the real joy of an amusement park, but eventually the ride ends.

The carousel metaphor is a good one for understanding three-act structure. What you really want to do is ride the racing horse around and around. But you start your day not at the carousel itself but at the park entrance. You've got a long way to go and many things to do—like buy tickets and wait your turn for the ride—before you can get what it is you came for. And then, no matter how many times you ride that thing, eventually you've got to get off and march back out to the car.

Riding the carousel is Act 2, the heart of the story. Act 1 is getting there, and Act 3 is heading home.

A clarification about Act 3: It's not just "the end." It isn't only getting off the ride after the fun is over. That's where the carousel metaphor breaks down. As I teach it, Act 3 includes the climax of the story and the dénouement. Act 3 takes everything to a precipice and then makes the hero take a leap. Act 3, the *leap*, is the high point of the action in the novel. After that climactic moment, you do have some tying off to do. That's the dénouement. So Act 3 is the leap and, if you will, the landing.

THE THREE-ACT STRUCTURE AND YOU

Think about your novel. Why are you writing it? What is the juicy goodness you taste whenever you think about this story? Maybe it's just the whole idea of the story that's fun, or maybe it's the genre you love. Perhaps it's the thrill of writing fiction at all. But after you've written a few of these, you'll begin craving a certain something about each book, or there's no point to do more than one. At that juncture, there's usually some kernel of an idea or feeling that you want to develop and display.

Chances are, that's what your Act 2 is going to be.

My sixth novel (*Operation: Firebrand—Deliverance*) is about an American covert ops team trying to find a North Korean family that wants to escape to China and beyond. The "fun" of that story idea was the team trying to help the family overcome their obstacles and win freedom. That's why I wrote that book. But I couldn't have started with my team in North Korea trying to get the family out. I had a lot of setup to do so I could get the game going. And then as the book neared its finish, I ultimately had to conclude their efforts for good or ill. So there was setup (Act 1) and final resolution (Act 3), but it was the exploration of their struggle (Act 2) that I most wanted to write about.

What is it for your book?

When you find that core idea, think about whether or not page 1 can feature this idea already in full swing. Probably not.

Probably you'll need to establish some things first. You'll need to introduce some people and show some situations so we'll be set up to understand your core idea. That's what will go in your Act 1.

And then cast your mind forward to how you might conclude the core idea. How will you bring it all to a head? With the time bomb ticking down and the villain about to do X and the hero's dreams about to collapse, how can you make it all smack together in a big finale? That, plus all the resolution you'll need to do to end everything nicely, is your Act 3.

You don't have to have it all set in stone before you write. But knowing in what direction you're heading on this road is an important determiner for how well-rounded your story will be when you write it.

❧ THREE-ACT STRUCTURE AND THE INNER JOURNEY ❧

Some of my language in this chapter may sound familiar to you. Earlier in the book I talked about the hero's inner journey, and some of the same ideas hold true there. You can't start a book with a character in the middle of his journey, for instance. You have some setup to do first, or we won't understand what's happening to her. That sounds like what I just said about how Act 1 has to do the setup so Act 2 can happen.

Indeed, there is much overlap between three-act structure and the main character's transformational arc. The two of them build upon and amplify one another. (This is the central premise of *Plot Versus Character*.)

The business of Act 1 is similar to the material I covered in chapter eight about the first phases of the inner journey: knot, initial condition, and inciting event. The escalation of the inner journey is roughly analogous to Act 2. And the hero's moment of truth and final state fall nicely into the climax and falling action of Act 3.

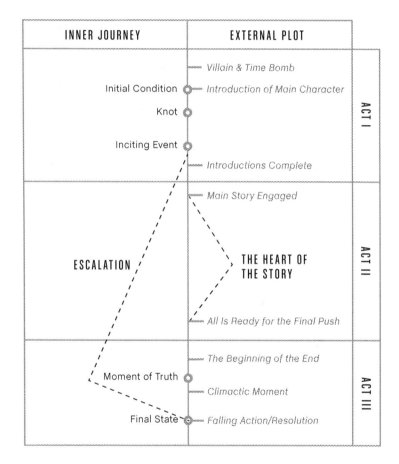

The heart of your protagonist's inner journey is what happens in the middle, which, not coincidentally, is what I've called the *heart* of your novel (Act 2).

Don't let this confuse you. Let it serve to crystallize your understanding of the tasks and structure a good novel will possess.

❧· ACT 1 ·❧

There is no set length for a novel's Act 1. Don't get locked into think-ing that Act 1 has to be one-third the length of your novel. Bah. It can be as long or as short as it needs to be. I've seen good Act 1s that are done in 35 pages, and I've seen good Act 1s that took 175 pages. Whenever you reach the point where the tasks for Act 1 are accomplished (which we'll talk about in a sec), Act 1 is done, and you can move on.

But it's safe to say that most of your first fifty pages will be con-cerned with the affairs of Act 1. So I'll proceed with a full discus-sion of what needs to happen in this first movement of your sym-phony, even if you end up needing more or fewer pages than fifty to get it all done.

What needs to happen in Act 1? We've already established that certain things have to be accomplished before Act 2 can begin. So that's one way to say it: Act 1 has to do everything that must be done so the fun and heart of the novel can happen.

And that's really the best answer. I'm going to get very specific about what elements must be covered in Act 1, but every novel is different, and yours may not fit nicely into what I'm saying. So when in doubt, go back to that more robust definition—Act 1 has to do everything that must be done so the fun and heart of the novel can happen—and you'll be set.

With that said, let's look at the components of a good Act 1. To be complete, your Act 1 must

1. introduce your major characters,
2. introduce the primary challenge or danger of the novel, and
3. get the hero to fully engage the main challenge of the story.

Let's talk about these one by one.

INTRODUCE YOUR MAJOR CHARACTERS

At the outset of this chapter, I said I wouldn't call Act 1 the beginning, but that I'd call it *introductions*. One of the most important tasks of Act 1, and of your first fifty pages, is to bring your main characters onstage. To introduce them to your reader.

We've already covered how to bring your protagonist onstage the first time. We've talked about creating a short story to reveal her essence. We've talked about showing how her knot is affecting her in her initial condition. And we've also looked at how to bring your villain onstage the first time.

Now it's time to round out the cast. Who else is a major player who has not yet been introduced? Will there be a love interest for the hero in this book? Better bring him on. Will there be one or more close friends? What about parents or bosses or team members? Anyone who is significant to the story needs to have some sort of introduction in Act 1.

Does that mean you can't introduce new characters in Act 2 or even Act 3? Absolutely not. You can bring on new characters on every page all the way to the last page, if you choose. But it does mean you have to introduce the prime movers early on in the story.

Here's why: No reader wants the climactic part of the novel to be decided—or even significantly affected—by some Johnny Come Lately we've just met. What if the climactic moment of *Casablanca* were resolved not by Rick, Ilsa, or Laszlo but by Floyd the air conditioner repair guy who just wandered onstage in time to save the day? Gah! What if the climax of *Jaws* were decided not by Brody, Quint, or Hooper but by some lifeguard with a harpoon gun? What?

If anyone is going to be important later in the story, we'd better have met her earlier in the story. During Act 1. Which very likely means during the first fifty pages.

One of the ways you can know you've completed Act 1 is when you see that you have introduced all the major players.

From this perspective only, when was Act 1 completed in *The Matrix*? When we'd met Neo, Trinity, Morpheus, and Agent Smith, at the least. Important other characters we needed to meet included Cypher, the Oracle, and the crew of the *Nebuchadnezzar*. When we'd seen all of these characters and gotten a sense of who they were and how they fit into the scheme of things, we could get on with the fun: Neo's rise to potency as a rival for the machines (which is Act 2).

What if we hadn't met Cypher until Act 2 or 3? He's the trickster/Judas character who sets the whole plot in motion. Such a pivotal character can't be stepping onstage just in time to do his pivoting. We need to have met him before. It's a principle you'll see me talking about time after time: Before we can comprehend the impact of something, we need to have had it set up for us. So it is with the main characters in your novel.

Who are those people in your book? Consider taking a minute right now to write down the name of each of your key characters and jotting down some ideas about how you might introduce each one. Keep in mind that these introductions will have to happen in the early portion of your novel. Not on page 1 for all of them, certainly, but probably by page 50.

Note that your smaller characters don't all need big standalone short stories to introduce them. Some might not need more than a memorable introductory paragraph. I just want you to consciously craft how each of these major and featured minor characters is first presented to the reader.

INTRODUCE THE PRIMARY CHALLENGE OR DANGER

Another main function of Act 1 is to let us know what this story is going to be about.

Before we can appreciate a team's wins on the field and struggles in the locker room, we have to have been shown that this is going to be a novel about a team of rugby players making an unlikely run for the World Cup (*Invictus*). Otherwise the victories would have no context, and thus no impact on the reader.

Act 1 orients the reader and puts him in the proper mindset to be able to receive what you want to do in Act 2.

That's true even for stories in which you want the reader *disoriented*. Consider the science fiction film *Pandorum*. The filmmakers wanted the audience just as confused as the hero is. He wakes up on an interstellar spaceship, but nothing is as he'd expected, and his own memory is faulty. The ship seems to be malfunctioning … and what are those strange sounds coming from outside this door that won't open?

But as the movie progresses, our hero learns bits and pieces of what's going on. And we learn it with him. Finally he realizes that he needs to get all the way across the ship to the reactor core to reset it before the ship shuts down completely. That journey, his quest to the core, is the heart of the movie (and quite thrilling, I might add, not least because of the ticking time bomb device the writers use). That's Act 2. Even though we were confused about what had transpired, we still learned a lot of information that oriented us in the story, so when he set out for the middle section of the story we knew what was going on and why.

That's your second task for Act 1: Give us a frame of reference with which we can comprehend what's going to happen in Act 2.

What is the primary challenge or danger in your novel? What's the main thing the hero is going to be doing in your book? Write that down in your notes.

The main thing Luke Skywalker is going to do is try to get the stolen schematics of the Death Star to Princess Leia so the Rebel Alliance can try to find a way to destroy it.

Indiana Jones's main task in *Raiders of the Lost Ark* is to try to find and save the Ark of the Covenant.

The primary thing Frodo will be doing is trying to get rid of the Ring so he and his loved ones can be safe from evil.

The main challenge of your story is the content of your plot. While your hero is undergoing personal challenges that will result in her coming to a moment of truth in her inner journey, she's also dealing with external story elements and characters who either aid or oppose her. This primary outer challenge has to be wound up and let loose in Act 1.

Knowing your story's main problem will help you map out what has to happen in your first fifty pages. When you know the main challenge the hero will face in Act 2, you can step backward to figure out what needs to be set up and in what order.

My third novel (*Fatal Defect*) is about a guy who tries to take down a terrorist organization that has used high-tech means to capture an island research facility to obtain a biological weapon of mass destruction. The whole fun was going to take place on the small atoll in the Pacific.

When I knew my main challenge, I realized I had some setup to do. I could step backward from that to find out what had to be put in place before the main action could happen. First, my hero didn't start on this island, so somehow I had to get him there. Second, I knew I needed to make him aware of the danger somehow, so I perceived I would have to figure out a way for the information to get to my hero. Then the terrorists would have to take over the island. Then we'd have to learn of their goals.

Do you see how knowing the main problem automatically builds your to-do list for Act 1? Again, this shouldn't feel like something that is stifling your creative process. These elements can be presented in any number of configurations. Just see them as helper clues to ensure you're including everything you need for the story to make sense.

How will the main danger or challenge of your novel intrude into your story? At some point early on, the characters (and readers) need to learn that the dam is in danger of bursting. Somewhere in the first fifty pages, the hero needs to find out that someone is out there killing people, and he must be stopped. When that is revealed, another main component of Act 1 is in place.

From this perspective, when was Act 1 completed in *Raiders of the Lost Ark*? When Indy learned that the Ark might be found and that the Nazis might get their hands on it. Because that's the main action of the movie.

Act 1 was over in *Music and Lyrics* when Alex is given a chance to revive his music career if he can write a song that will be accepted by pop star Cora Corman.

When was Act 1 done in *Avatar*? When Jake meets Neytiri and begins having his paradigm shifted about the worth of this culture and the justness of his army's cause.

At the point when you have established the main challenge of your story, you have accomplished the second task for an excellent Act 1.

THE INTRUSION

When we looked at the hero's inner journey, we talked about the inciting event, the thing that comes into his unhealthy but "normal" life and sends him careening down a detour that will lead eventually to his moment of truth. There's something similar to that in three-act structure. I call it the *intrusion*. This is when the main danger or challenge of the story finally crashes into the hero's world.

The two are closely related, but not identical. Sometimes they happen at the same moment and even as part of the same event, but they have different purposes, so I think it's worth speaking about them separately.

In *Casablanca*, the primary problem of the story intrudes into Rick's life when Ilsa walks into Rick's Café Américain. This triggers a series of events that will lead to a radical change in our hero's external situation. Note that this is also the inciting event for his inner journey.

But the inciting event and the intrusion are not always one and the same. At the beginning of my fourth novel (*Operation: Firebrand*), the hero, Jason, is a Navy SEAL. A mission goes wrong, and his best friend is severely wounded. Jason leaves the Navy and commences to heap punishment on himself for what happened. The intrusion of the main challenge in the story is when he is recruited to lead a privately funded covert ops team. This begins the primary plot action of the book.

But it isn't until later, when out on a mission with this new team, that Jason's inciting event takes place in his inner journey. He encounters someone who gives him a reason to live—and to care again. Now he's struggling internally against his guilt, and meanwhile he's in a combat zone struggling externally as well.

See how the inciting event and the intrusion have different functions? It's fine if the two happen simultaneously. They most often do, but they don't have to. Just be sure to give both of them some careful thought.

THE HERO TAKES THE CHALLENGE

The final component of a complete Act 1 is causing the protagonist to fully engage the main problem of the story.

It's vital to introduce the main players and show us what the story is going to be about, but until the hero commits to doing something about it, it's all just academic.

Dorothy might have gotten to Oz and met the key players and learned that she needs to see the Wizard if she hopes to get home, but until she sets out along the yellow brick road, it means nothing.

The story doesn't begin in earnest until the hero vows to go. To try. To rise up and fight.

Milo Thatch wanted to try to discover Atlantis. He'd been given the means and had met the people who could make it happen, but until he got on the submersible, it was just a thought experiment.

William Wallace hated the English and loved his native Scotland (in *Braveheart*). He saw the dangers and had comrades-in-arms around him. But until he decided to actively oppose the invaders, the story had not truly begun.

Many times, it is the hero deciding to accept the challenge of the story. Captain John Miller (Tom Hanks's character in *Saving Private Ryan*) accepts orders to find Private Ryan and get him safely home. The Three Amigos draw a line in the sand and step over it, indicating their willingness to try to undo the mess they've made of things. Milo Thatch gets on the sub.

But sometimes it is the story that engages the hero, instead of the other way around. William Wallace could've lived many more years under English rule had an Englishman not killed Wallace's bride. But that pushed him over the limit. Frodo never asked to become a hero, but the story had other plans. It would not let him stay comfortable. Luke Skywalker said he wanted to fight the Empire, but when his opportunity came, he balked. "Fate" had to come along and kill his family in order to shove him into action.

One way or another, your hero will engage the main challenge of the story. Either she'll raise her hand to volunteer or she'll find herself unwittingly volunteered. Either way, she'll become caught up in the action, and the fun can begin.

This aspect of Act 1 represents the transition point between Act 1 and Act 2. When the main action is fully engaged, the other two parts (introducing the characters and establishing the primary challenge) had better already be in place, because now the game is on.

From this perspective only, when did Act 1 end in *Ice Age*? When Manny decided he would get personally involved in protecting the human baby and trying to return him to his tribe.

When did Act 1 end in *Mulan*? When Mulan cuts her hair, disguises herself as a man, and rides off secretly to join the army in place of her father. She fully engaged the main action of the story.

When did Act 1 end in *Aliens*? When most of the platoon is killed by the creatures and the soldiers' way back to the main ship is destroyed. Now they are stuck on the planet, where they will be forced into a battle to the death with the aliens. The main story engaged them.

What will this pivot point be for your book? You know your main characters and the chief task of the book, but at what point will your hero become well and truly enmeshed in it?

❧· THE STEW ·❧

Your first fifty pages are chock full of good stuff, aren't they? Maybe more than you'd ever thought about. It may even seem that I've got an unending number of things to talk about, each one an essential element that must be included in these pages—or else.

Well, don't stress about it. Don't see these as laws or do-or-die elements that have to be in your book or the novel will die. As a friend of mine says: they're tools, not rules. See them more as suggestions, best practices that can possibly give you ideas that will help your first fifty pages be as strong as they can be and achieve all your objectives for how your novel begins.

Let's pull together the three components of a strong Act 1. Get your own story in mind, and then consider these questions:

- **WHO ARE THE MAIN CHARACTERS IN YOUR NOVEL?** Who are the "playas," the ones who affect the story? How will you introduce each one? Your Act 1 is not complete until you've let us meet and get to know them. When we do know them, they can be set free to dance their dance.

- **WHAT IS THE MAIN CHALLENGE OF YOUR NOVEL?** What's happening that is going to disrupt your hero's life and occupy all her energies for the duration of the story? Act 1 is not complete until we've seen what the main problem is. When we do know it, we're ready for something to be done about it.

- **HOW WILL YOUR HERO BECOME FULLY ENGAGED WITH THIS MAIN CHALLENGE?** Either your protagonist is going to leave home and strike out toward the Cracks of Doom or the story is going to reach out and begin pulling him inexorably toward a fatal showdown. Your Act 1 is not complete—indeed, Act 2 cannot begin—until the hero has jumped into (or been thrown into) the bubbling vat that is your main story.

When have all three of these components been accomplished in *Star Trek* (2009)? Well, within the first several scenes we've met James T. Kirk, "Bones," Spock, and the rest of the people who will become our iconic bridge crew. And we've seen the Romulan ship on a mission of destruction, which becomes the main challenge of the story. The heart of the movie, its Act 2, is the race to save Earth from annihilation. So certain things have to be set up before that can begin. Finally, when the *Enterprise* goes to warp to respond to an emergency on Vulcan—and Kirk storms onto the bridge to warn of what's about to happen—Act 1 has ended and Act 2 can begin. Everyone is in place, we know the danger, and the main action is engaged.

In *The Little Mermaid*, when has Act 1 ended? It has to be sometime after all the main characters have been introduced, so we have to have met Ariel, Flounder, King Triton, Eric, Scuttle, Sebastian, and of course Ursula, the sea witch. And it has to be when the main challenge has been introduced. In this case, the main challenge is Ariel's desire to pursue a romance with Eric, who is a regular human, a prospect that is forbidden by her father, king of the merpeople. Finally, Act 1 can end when the hero has engaged the main challenge. That happens in this movie when Ariel goes to Ursula and agrees to a terrible bargain in which she will receive human legs. When she does this, and when she washes up on shore and meets Eric, Act 1 has ended and the real fun can begin.

What will it be in your story?

As you contemplate this large project you're going to begin, trace out the broad strokes that constitute a good three-act structure. Then look closely at what needs to go into your Act 1.

See this as a fun exercise. You're putting all these excellent ingredients into a stew, and you can be sure the result will be delicious. Have a blast just asking questions at this point—How will I introduce my hero's best friend? What's a cool way to first hint that something scary is going to happen?—and writing down possible answers. At the end of this book, you'll put it on the fire to simmer. Let it cook awhile before beginning to ladle out specific servings.

CHAPTER 12

THE FIRST PAGE

"Where shall I begin, please your Majesty?" he asked.
"Begin at the beginning," the King said, gravely, "and go on till you
come to the end: then stop." –LEWIS CARROLL

I HAVE PURPOSELY WAITED UNTIL NEAR THE END OF this book to talk about the words you will use to actually begin your novel. That may seem backward. I mean, why not start with how to create your own "Call me Ishmael" and build from there?

Because if you did it that way, you could write an amazing first line and a terrific first page ... and then have to throw them out when you learned all the other things about how your novel should begin. It's a lot easier to come up with a great first line and first page than it is to fix a beginning that is structured wrong or fails to accomplish the tasks it should. Better to get the main things right and then come back and find the ideal way to begin *that*.

In this chapter we're going to look at how to craft your opening line, how to continue it to a great opening page, and then how to extend that out for the next forty-nine pages.

How exactly do you want to begin your book?

Before you begin thinking about opening lines, pull out your notes and start synthesizing everything you've learned in this book so far. Your novel's first line is the tip of the proverbial iceberg. It's the first visible facet of something big that can't be detected yet. Nevertheless, it is a part of that still-invisible thing. If you were to be able to see the whole mass at once, you would see how this top part fits and is a logical outgrowth of the rest.

The first line "grows" from the larger construct of your novel's first fifty pages. So before you write your first line and your first page, figure out if you want to start with a prologue or *in media res* or whatever else. Have the scene pretty well plotted out, at least to the point that you know what things you want to accomplish with the opening segment. Then when you sit down to write that opening line, you'll have a grip on what it's leading to.

❧· YOUR FIRST LINE ·❧

In a real sense, your novel's opening line is a come-on line. With just a handful of words, you're trying to keep your reader from going back to whatever she was doing. You want her to commit to your story, forsaking all others—at least until she reaches the end. She's heard hundreds of these pick-up lines before, and a lame one may just be the last time she listens to you. So make it a good one.

> "Happy families are all alike; every unhappy family is unhappy in its own way"—Leo Tolstoy, *Anna Karenina*.

> "It was the best of times, it was the worst of times"—Charles Dickens, *A Tale of Two Cities*.

> "You don't know about me without you have read a book by the name of The Adventures of Tom Sawyer; but that ain't no matter"—Mark Twain, *The Adventures of Huckleberry Finn*.

> "It is a truth universally acknowledged, that a single man in possession of a good fortune, must be in want of a wife"—Jane Austen, *Pride and Prejudice*.

And of course,

"Call me Ishmael"—Herman Melville, *Moby-Dick.*

Plus, we should not forget the infamous first line from Edward George Bulwer-Lytton's 1830 novel, *Paul Clifford*: "It was a dark and stormy night." No, really. It's not a cliché when you're the first to write it.

I told you about my trip to the library in which I pulled several novels from the new releases shelf and read the first line of each, looking for one that grabbed me. Most did not.

Now, many readers—maybe most readers—won't have such a stringent entrance exam. In our day of cheap e-books, readers tend to buy an entire book based on price alone, and only later … maybe … actually try to read it.

But whether your first line is part of what causes someone to buy your book or not, it is something that will impact his decision to *read* your book or not.

The first line of a novel has an impact that exceeds perhaps every other line in the book. There may be crucial, even life-changing moments later in your novel, but in terms of spots we can point to in every work of fiction, the first line is paramount. It resonates through the corridors of the rest of the work. It has the power to set tone and expectation. It is the first thing that orients the reader to the world of your story, rather like the tour guide who meets you at the edge of the ancient monument you're about to tour.

What makes a first line good or bad? Certainly there's no formula, as demonstrated by the sampling of opening lines shown above. Nevertheless, there are guidelines that, if adhered to, will result in a great first line.

Your novel's opening line should be *simple, engaging,* and *appropriate for the tone of your book.*

Meet these three conditions, and your novel will begin well. No one can promise it will be an immortal first line, and whether or not it will succeed as a pick-up line is out of everyone's control. But I can at least guarantee that it will be a solid opening that will get your novel off to a strong start.

YOUR FIRST LINE MUST BE SIMPLE

> The bone-chilling scream split the warm summer night in two, the first half being before the scream when it was fairly balmy and calm and pleasant for those who hadn't heard the scream at all, but not calm or balmy or even very nice for those who did hear the scream, discounting the little period of time during the actual scream itself when your ears might have been hearing it but your brain wasn't reacting yet to let you know.

When you're trying to write badly, as Patricia E. Presutti was when she wrote the above to earn the dubious honor of winning the 1986 Bulwer-Lytton Fiction Contest for worst first lines in fiction, it's okay to have an opening sentence like that one. (Isn't it beautifully awful?) But when you're not trying to write poorly, you'll want to go with something simpler.

Why is it important to keep things simple? Readers are looking for easy access into a new novel. Psychologically, they want to find a quick handhold that can make them feel like this is an ascent they can make quick progress upon. For your part, as the author, you want to get them through the door and on to the inner rooms as fast and as painlessly as possible. Put a Slip-n-Slide over your threshold. Not a barricade.

If you begin with a complex, obtuse sentence, you're laying a roadblock before the reader's tires. You're saying, "Don't read me. I'm going to be hard to understand. You're going to have to work very hard to get through this thing. Probably better for you to look elsewhere."

I'm guessing that's not the message you're hoping to convey to your reader. You probably do want him to come inside and enjoy the wonder you've created for him. So don't try to do too much with that opening line. Remember to K.I.S.S.—keep it simple, soldier.

By "simple" I mean it should be pretty short—no more than one or two lines in length—and it should flow easily. Try to avoid parenthetical phrases or even commas. Skip the impressive vocabulary. Make it a nice, legato sentence with a single thought.

If you haven't yet written your opening line, you're fine so far. Just keep it simple when you do sit down to write it. I know novelists who wait until they've written their entire rough draft before coming back and writing the opening line. That makes sense to me. You may not know the perfect first line until you've written your last line. Even if you do write a first line first, remember to come back to it in revisions and see if it's the very best it can be.

If you *have* already written your novel's first line, take a look at it now. Is it simple?

Your opening sentence can be a line of dialogue, a description, or a thought. It can be any element of fiction, actually. Just make sure it doesn't cause the reader to stumble, and you'll be on your way to making it a great first line.

THE FIRST LINE MUST BE ENGAGING

In addition to being a breeze and a joy to read, your opening line must also be engaging. It must be interesting. Every sentence in your novel will serve some purpose, of course, or you'd cut it. So in a sense, you hope every line is interesting. But a first sentence must be intriguing in an objective sense.

Remember, the reader is coming from her own world of taxes, bills, kids, and a car that doesn't work. And she's got a thousand other entertainment choices vying for her attention. Except for your mom, no reader is going to read your novel simply because you wrote it. The rest of the potential readers out there are free agents able to read or do anything they please with these next minutes or hours. Part of whether or not she spends it with your book hinges on your first line being a grabber.

A grabber not in the sense that it's a great fit with your other lines around it, because thus far the reader has seen no other lines from your book. This one has to be interesting, as I said, in an objective sense. If your opening line were taken from your book and sent out on Twitter, it would have to stand alone as interesting in and of itself.

In a way, your opening line is your whole book in microcosm. It is the shortest of short stories. It is the one representative you send from the village to go petition the king. So you have to make it interesting.

That doesn't mean something interesting has to happen in the first line, like, "He pulled the trigger." Well, that actually would be a pretty good first line, I think, but my point remains that it doesn't have to talk about inherently interesting actions. The sentence itself has to be fascinating, but the content expressed does not. As "Call me Ishmael" attests.

If Job One is to engage your reader, then Part AAA-0001 of that is to write an engaging opening line. Let's take a look at how to do that effectively.

WHAT MAKES A FIRST LINE ENGAGING

What kind of opening sentence would engage a reader?

I have found these four categories to be most effective:

1. Make it striking
2. Make it profound
3. Make it funny
4. Make it mysterious

An example of a striking opening line is the one from my first novel (*Virtually Eliminated*): "Once he decided to kill himself, the rest was easy."

Here's another: "I stare down at my shoes, watching as a fine layer of ash settles on the worn leather." That striking first line is from *Mockingjay* by Suzanne Collins.

"Gestures are all that I have; sometimes they must be grand in nature." That's how Garth Stein's *The Art of Racing in the Rain* begins. The narrator is actually a dog, which is an interesting premise. Now, I personally wish the editor had made that opening line into two sentences and cut a word. I think it would've been even more striking as "Gestures are all I have." But it's still quite good.

Another way to make an opening line striking is to let it be a bit of dialogue or internal monologue from a character who speaks with a unique voice. That's how Mark Twain succeeded so well with "You don't know about me without you have read a book by the name of *The Adventures of Tom Sawyer*; but that ain't no matter."

Think about your book. Can you think of something surprising and fresh and unusual to say as the opening line? It might be the way to go for you. Just remember to also keep it simple.

Or you could work to make your opening line *profound*. Tolstoy nailed this kind of first line with "Happy families are all alike;

every unhappy family is unhappy in its own way." It's a thoughtful presentation of the philosophical theme we're going to be exploring in the novel. Could your book begin with a statement like that? If you know your theme, brainstorm a handful of proverb-like opening lines. Maybe you'll strike gold.

You could also try to make your opening line *funny*. Note that this should be done only if you're writing a novel with a humorous or at least wry bent. Technically, this example is cheating because it's two sentences, but it's one comic beat: "Dawn poked her rosy fingers across the sky. And promptly tore two small holes in it." That's how *Hero, Second Class* by Mitchell Bonds begins.

Here's how *A Total Waste of Makeup* by Kim Gruenenfelder begins: "Okay, so when my great-grandniece reads this, it's probably going to be, like, 2106, and by then there will not only be pagers, cell phones, e-mail, and answering machines, but some necklace that can reach you at any time, day or night." Now, that's not exactly simple, but it is fun to read and it implies a humorous time to come.

If your book is a comedy or has a comic voice, consider a humorous opening line.

Another great approach is to make your first line *mysterious*. Something intriguing. Something that simply won't let the reader stop there.

Consider how Kimberly Stuart begins *Operation Bonnet*: "I didn't set out to be the town luminary." Now wait: The town luminary—what could that mean? Obviously something happened that the narrator wasn't expecting. What was it? Maybe you could resist reading at least a little more of that book, but I couldn't. Notice also that it's a simple sentence. That's part of its strength.

"Maybe it isn't fair, but I blame Karen Vogel for what just happened." That's how John Locke begins *Saving Rachel*. See how that generates a question in your mind: Whoa, what *did* just happen?

"I knew what was coming as soon as he handed me the teddy bear"—*Fashionably Late* by Beth Kendrick. Intriguing first line.

Use care not only in what words you use in your opening sentence but in what you choose to talk about in it. I saw an unpublished novel once that began by telling me how boring the day was. That's not going to engage your reader, believe me. And here's how Maeve Binchy begins *Minding Frankie*: "Katie Finglas was coming to the end of a tiring day in the salon." Don't do that. I'm sure Binchy has written a great novel, but I can't help thinking that another first line would've served her better. If you tell your reader right away that this book begins in a boring way, she may believe you … and go look for a more entertaining book to read.

When you think about how to make your opening line engaging, keep these four approaches in mind. Why not try all four, each one several times, until you hit upon one you like best?

YOUR FIRST LINE MUST BE APPROPRIATE FOR THE TONE OF YOUR BOOK

Your opening sentence is one of your most powerful tools for setting the tone of your novel. So you should choose it carefully.

I mentioned above that if you're writing a serious novel, you shouldn't begin with a humorous first line. The same goes for other kinds of novels. If you're writing something akin to *Black Hawk Down*, you probably shouldn't begin with an anecdote about planting rose bushes. If you're writing a romantic comedy, a first line about disemboweling a pig is not going to set the right mood.

Be conscious of your first line. It's something that should be chosen, not settled for. You can jot down the first thing that comes into your mind and leave it there for now, because I certainly don't want you paralyzed for weeks as you stress over crafting just the right first line. Sometimes it's good just to write anything down and keep forging ahead. But be sure to come back later and take another run at that opening sentence.

Step back from your book idea a minute. If you had to give one word or phrase that described the mood of your book, what would you say? What's the voice and tone? Is it snarky? Is it an unflinching exploration inside the mind of a mass murderer? Is it sardonic? Is it carefree? Is it blissful?

When you have your book's mood in mind, you also have found the mood you should set with your opening line.

I told you my first opening sentence, "Once I decided to kill myself, the rest was easy." Okay, well, that wouldn't work if it were a light romance about freewheeling teens on spring break at Port Aransas. If that line is going to work, it will be for a novel that would have room for a narrator character intent upon committing suicide—and doing who knows what before then. Which it does.

What about your novel? What's the overall tone? Make sure your opening line does not mislead the reader about what kind of book it's going to be. Remember that this is your first and most powerful means of getting your reader oriented and headed in the right direction so he can best appreciate what you're doing in the rest of your novel.

LET'S ANALYZE SOME FIRST LINES

All of these are picked from novels that were Amazon.com bestsellers at the time of this writing, so it goes to show that you can write a good first line or a lousy first line and still end up at the top. But if you can choose a good first line, you probably should.

Armed with the knowledge that a first line ought to be simple, engaging, and appropriate for the tone of the novel, what do you think of these?

"The band of travelers walked along the path between the clear sparkling water of Grass River and the black-streaked white limestone cliff, following the trail that paralleled the right bank." It's from *The Land of Painted Caves* by Jean M. Auel.

Again, this is from a best-selling book, so who am I to say it should've been done differently? But this first line is neither simple nor engaging. With apologies to the author, it's a snoozer. It would not pass my library test. Is it appropriate for the tone of the book? Well, I don't know, but since the first line seems kind of dull, I'm thinking it doesn't match the rest of the book or it probably wouldn't be selling so well. You want your book to succeed in part because of your first line, not in spite of it.

How about this one, which is from *Sweet Valley Confidential: Ten Years Later* by Francine Pascal? "Elizabeth had turned the key in the Fox lock, releasing a heavy metal bar that scraped across the inside of the front door with an impressive prison-gate sound, and was about to attack the Segal lock when the phone in the apartment started to ring."

Hoo. Well, it doesn't pass the simple test. I'd say the author was trying to do too much with one sentence, especially her first one. But it is rather interesting, and we can give her the benefit of the doubt that it fits the tone of the rest of the book. I'd want her to simplify it, like maybe start with, "Great—just great," or some other line of dialogue as a grabber before giving that bigger sentence next. Remember, lay out the Slip-n-Slide. Get that reader quickly into the interior of your book.

How's this one? "One sunny, crisp Saturday in September when I was seven years old, I watched my father drop dead." I like this one. I think it could be simplified to do less in one sentence, but it's quite engaging. I'm hooked. That's how Jodi Picoult begins *Sing You Home*.

Here's one from a novel I edited: "The dark man was back." Fresh and intriguing, I think. Definitely simple and appropriate for what comes next. It's from *The Dark Man* by Marc Schooley.

"The forty days of the soul begin on the morning after death." Ooh, I want to read more. It's simple and engaging and, we trust, appropriate for the mood of the book. That's how Teá Obreht begins *The Tiger's Wife*.

All right, I think you're equipped now. But now you're spoiled for mediocre novel openings. Sorry.

(And … don't start by someone getting out of a car, okay? Or having a dream that she'll then wake up from.)

If you do your opening line correctly, you will hook your reader. It will be a great pick-up line—for at least the first page. And if it does that, your first line has accomplished its purpose. Even the best opening sentence won't hold a reader for the duration of a novel, especially a poorly written novel. But it will hang on to his interest long enough to get him down the first page, where your other great lines can continue to pull him in.

❧• YOUR FIRST PAGE •❧

The first page is the interface between that great opening line and the rest of your novel. You've crafted a terrific one-liner to begin the novel, but the reader might be suspecting that that line might've been a special case, a ringer brought in just to snag her interest. Now you've got to actually start unspooling this yarn. If the first line got her on the hook, the first page will determine whether or not it sets or if the fish throws the hook and gets away.

By this point in *The First 50 Pages* you've given a lot of thought to how your novel will begin. You've probably got a pretty good idea of the structure you'll give your opening, and you certainly have a shopping list of elements you'll need to work into those first pages by hook or by crook. Now that you've also considered what your opening line must be, it's time to hitch that to the front end of the rest of the novel.

It (almost) goes without saying that your first page needs to be interesting. Job One, you'll recall, is to engage your reader. That task extends for the entire first fifty pages, not just your opening sentence.

I can't tell you how many unpublished manuscripts I've seen that begin with a decent first line and then launch into a page or more of backstory or other forms of telling. A great first line buys you about two more sentences of reader engagement. If you don't follow it up pretty quickly with more interesting content, you'll lose her.

Your first page is not the place to explain everything. (Indeed, if we're talking outright telling, the first *fifty* pages are not the place for it.) The first page is the place to engage your reader.

In part one I talked about the need to give description of your setting fairly early in any new scene. I said this description should've begun somewhere by the second half of the first page. So what is it that should go between 1) the amazing opening line and 2) the beginning of your description of the setting? Why, something interesting, of course!

Let's see it done well. Here's the opening page of *Love You More* by Lisa Gardner (note that in the original this is all set in italics):

Who do you love?

It's a question anyone should be able to answer. A question that defines a life, creates a future, guides most minutes of one's days. Simple, elegant, encompassing.

Who do you love?

He asked the question, and I felt the answer in the weight of my duty belt, the constrictive confines of my armored vest, the tight brim of my trooper's hat, pulled low over my brow. I reached down slowly, my fingers just brushing the top of my Sig Sauer, holstered at my hip.

"Who do you love?" he cried again, louder now, more insistent.

My fingers bypassed my state-issued weapon, finding the black leather keeper that held my duty belt to my waist. The Velcro rasped loudly as I unfastened the first band, then the second, third, fourth. I worked the metal buckle, then my twenty pound duty belt, complete with my sidearm, Taser, and collapsible steel baton released from my waist and dangled in the space between us.

"Don't do this," I whispered, one last shot at reason.

He merely smiled. "Too little, too late."

"Where's Sophie? What did you do?"

"Belt. On the table. Now."

"No."

"GUN. On the table. NOW!"

In response, I widened my stance, squaring off in the middle of the kitchen, duty belt still suspended from my left hand.

Okay, what do you think? How do you like her first line? Pretty great, I think. Simple, engaging, and appropriate for the tone of what comes next. Then jump down to the bottom of the page. See her beginning to give us a sense of where this is taking place? I would personally prefer more description to give me a better feel for this setting, but at least I've got "kitchen" to work with.

What's in between? Between those is Gardner's deft means of continuing to reel us in. This is a tense standoff between a policeman and a gunman. For some bizarre reason (bizarre enough for us to want to keep reading to find out why), the cop is obeying the bad guy's commands. What's going on here? I don't know, but I want to find out.

Now that's a great first page.

See the pattern: good opening line, interesting thing happening (with not one bit of exposition), and then description of the setting before the end of the page.

Let's examine another:

> Like the luxury co-ops and five-star French eateries located in Manhattan's Silk Stocking District, Benchley East Side Parking was outrageously exclusive. Tucked side by side and bumper to bumper within its four temperature-controlled underground levels beneath East 77th Street were several vintage Porsches, a handful of Ferraris, even a pair of his-and-her Lamborghinis.
>
> The out-of-the-box midnight blue SL550 Mercedes convertible that squealed out of its car elevator at three minutes past noon that Saturday seemed tailor-fit to the high-rent neighborhood.
>
> So did the lean forty-something waiting by the garage's office when the sleek Merc stopped on a dime out front.
>
> With his salt-and-pepper Beckham buzz cut, pressed khakis, silk navy golf shirt, and deep golden tan that suggested even deeper pockets, it was hard to tell if the car or its driver was being described by the purring Merc's vanity plate:
>
> SXY BST
>
> "With this heat, I figured you'd want the top down, as usual, Mr. Berger," the smiling half-Hispanic, half-Asian garage attendant

> said as he bounced out and held open the wood-inlaid door.
> "Have a good one, now."
>
> "Thanks, Tommy," Berger said, deftly slipping the man a five as
> he slid behind the luxury sports car's iconic three-pronged steer-
> ing wheel. "I'll give it a shot."

All right, let's talk about it. Since it's written by massively best-selling author James Patterson (with Michael Ledwidge), we're going to
assume that *Tick Tock* is a terrific novel that will sell a jillion copies.
So, with that in mind, and meaning no disrespect to the authors,
let's peek under this bad boy's hood.

What do you think of the opening line? It's not particularly
simple. I stumbled over it the first time I read it. It's a mouthful.
Nor is it especially interesting. Being that it's about expensive cars,
and the book is probably going to be about those cars and their
owners, we'll assume it's appropriate. So the first sentence could've
been stronger.

What about description? We're getting that from the first line,
so there's no concerns that we won't have enough by the end of the
first page. Got that covered.

But remember Job One. What should come between a great first
line and the description of the setting is something very interesting that will engage the reader. Now, Patterson's readers will keep
going, knowing that things will get exciting later. But we shouldn't
ever ask our reader to endure the boring stuff to get to the fun. It
should all be fun—especially on the first page. If I were the editor
on this book, I would've asked that the authors go take another
shot at this opening.

One more:

> Rough stone tore Rathe's palms as he stumbled through the gap-
> ing maw of the cave. He tore away the makeshift leaf filter cover-

ing his mouth and sucked in the cool underground air, soothing his burning lungs. Pain lanced through his side as each breath tortured cracked ribs.

He turned to the entrance and gazed into the ash-clogged air outside. Grey blanketed the world like a shroud, quickly swallowing his large three-toed tracks and obliterating any scent that would lead the trackers to him. Satisfied that he would be safe for the duration of the ash fall, Rathe staggered farther into the cave. His claws echoed hollowly on the stone floor, their quiet *clack, clack, clack* bouncing into the darkness.

The musical trickle of water sounded nearby, and Rathe angled toward it. Sudden wetness at his feet alerted him to the presence of a shallow pool. He lowered gingerly to the ground and stuck his snout into the chill liquid. The bitter taste of ash flowed over his tongue, but sweet relief filled his parched throat. Yet each swallow intensified the pain in his ribs.

The cool, moist rock felt good against his hot skin. He rolled onto his left side, away from the fire in his battered ribs, and stretched out to his full twelve-foot length. His tail-tip lazily slapped against the ground as drowsiness flowed over him. The water's flow sung him to sleep.

A shrill cry jolted Rathe from soothing darkness. Pain seared through his right side and down his tail. Through the agony, the fading echo of the cry played at the edges of his mind. He groaned as he rolled onto his belly and forced down a few more swallows of water.

He pushed to his feet, swaying slightly as his stiff muscles adjusted to his weight. He cocked his head and listened.

Whatever had made the sound had gone silent. Or the cry had been only the vestige of a nightmare.

So begins *Starfire* by Stuart Vaughn Stockton. The first line is simple, engaging, and appropriate for what comes next. We get a good description of this setting, including sensory information. And are we engaged by the rest of page 1? Well, if you might like a story about a twelve-foot-long sentient creature with three-toed feet and a long tail (and, really, who wouldn't?), you'd have to answer yes.

If you've yet to write your book's first page, you know how to do it now. The interesting middle (between great first line and description of the setting) can be just about anything you want— dialogue, action, even interior monologue, if it's brilliant—so long as it's interesting and serves to hook your reader.

If you've already written the first page, now you know how to dissect it to see if it's working well to help you keep the reader on that hook.

❧ THE RIGHT HOOK ❧

Your novel's first page will probably look pretty easy to the reader. It's just one page, after all. That's nothing compared to writing a whole book. True. But a great first page is really the culmination of a whole boatload of careful thought.

It has to engage, of course. But it also has to orient the reader to what kind of novel this is going to be. It has to be the correct beginning for *this* novel. Depending on how you order your book, the first page may introduce the hero or the villain. It may start us in a prologue years before the main story or it may put us at the very edge of the final precipice, or somewhere in between.

The first page is the tip of the spear of your book, and the first line is the bleeding edge of the tip of the spear. Not that we're trying to harpoon our readers. Maybe "hook" is the better metaphor.

When you go angling to catch a reader, choose the right hook and the right bait. Fish the hole just right, and you may find yourself with something on the line.

CHAPTER 13
PAGES 2 TO 50

There will come a time when you believe everything is finished.
That will be the beginning. **—LOUIS L'AMOUR**

BETWEEN YOUR STELLAR OPENING LINE AND FIRST page and the outermost perimeter of this book's scope (or the bottom of page 50, whichever comes first) lie forty-nine pages of fun.

It's dizzying, isn't it, how much your first fifty pages will accomplish. Hopefully you're not thinking, "I understood all this … until you explained it." You've learned the equivalent of a college course's worth of material on this subject. Indeed, you're now as much an expert on how to begin a novel as just about anyone else.

In this, our final chapter together, I'm going to talk about everything that hasn't come up yet on the topic—multiple storylines, dual protagonists, theme, circularity, and more. So stay with me for a few more pages, and let's land this plane.

STICK WITH YOUR MAIN STORY LINE FOR THE FIRST FORTY PAGES

In all our discussion of your first fifty pages, I have only lightly touched on a significant issue pertaining to your book's beginning: multiple story lines and viewpoint characters.

I believe you must *stick with your main protagonist for the first forty contiguous pages of your novel.*

Outside of a prologue, which is a freebie that can feature any other character or story line, once you bring your main character onstage, we readers need to stay with her for roughly forty pages in a row before you cut away to other story lines and viewpoint characters.

Though I haven't mentioned this until now, it lines up with everything else I've said. In the first fifty pages, you're establishing the hero's initial state and knot, so of course she needs to be onstage for that. You're also working to engage the reader in an intimate connection with the hero, so she needs to be onstage for that. You're showing the protagonist's work and home and other aspects of her "normal," so she needs to be onstage for that. Just about everything else we've talked about in this book requires the hero to be on the stage of the story in these first fifty pages.

Nevertheless, it's possible that you are surprised by what I'm saying right now. And if you've already written the first fifty-plus pages of your novel, you may not have done it this way. I'm asking you to please consider reworking it so your protagonist is who we're looking at for at least forty pages in a row.

Here's why.

When your reader begins your novel, he is not connected with it or any of your characters. Unless this is a sequel, he probably has no preexisting knowledge of your hero. He's coming to your book cold.

It will take a minute—er, several pages—for him to begin to get oriented into your book. For the reader, beginning a new novel is like being teleported into some alternate dimension. It's going to take some time to look around, get his bearings, and discern the lay of the land. After a while, though, if you've done your job right, the disorientation will wear off and he'll be ready to go with you on any adventure.

You help your reader make this adjustment by giving him continuity. You introduce him to one main character, and you proceed to let him look over that character's shoulder for a good long time before jumping away to some new character. Your reader watches this main character and begins to get a feel for being inside that person's skin and head. The reader starts to feel at home—and, more importantly, begins to grow a bond with that character. Which, as I may have mentioned already, is Job One.

Contrast that with the kind of thing I see in unpublished (and far too many published) manuscripts, in which the author jumps from story line to story line like a flea on a dog getting a bath.

I've seen novels in which I'm in seventeen story lines and viewpoint characters before I hit page 50. It's maddening. We go two pages in Mildred's head and begin learning about her life and personality and situation, but then at the bottom of page 2 we jump to Aziz's head as he runs toward a water mirage in the desert. Just as we're beginning to get a sense for Aziz, we're yanked over to Sylvester, who is foreclosing on his granddaughter's home. We're trying to figure out why someone would do this, but now we're yanked over to Linda's apartment in Brazil, where she's contemplating leaving her cheating husband. Like Linda? Too bad, because now you must meet Bubba, then Pierre, then Trieu, then the UCLA table tennis team … By the time we get back around to Mildred, we have no clue who that person was.

Worse, we don't care.

Your reader desperately wants to connect with your hero and your story. It's why she's come to your novel in the first place: She wants to find a likable person with whom to go on an entertaining ride.

But when you pull her away from your hero before she has made a strong connection, you actually sever what connection was there. Because now she has to start over again with a new character and his life situation. Whatever engagement she'd had with Character A is now diffused to the wind, and she begins trying to connect with Character B. But she has less energy for doing that, because she'd already given her love to Character A.

And every additional time you cut to yet another character's life, you break the connection again. Each time this happens, the reader has less energy to devote to starting over with someone new. Until there's no energy at all, and no connection at all. That's when she puts your book down and goes to see what's on TV.

Authors jump like this, I think, because they want to show the variety the reader is going to experience during the course of the novel, or possibly in a frantic attempt to engage the reader. Maybe you won't like Character A, so I'll show you Characters B through Z in a quick parade. Surely you'll like one of them. But this actually has the opposite effect. Every time you cut to a new viewpoint character in those first fifty pages, you actively *prevent* the reader from connecting to any of them.

Don't do this. Trust that what you've done to make your hero likable and engaging will work (reread chapter four for a refresher), and stay with him for forty pages in a row.

Now, am I saying your book can't have multiple viewpoint characters? Nay, I say. You can have several viewpoint characters in your novel (but probably not more than six or seven in a typical novel). What I am saying is that you need to let us fully connect with your *main character* before asking us to care about anyone else.

When you've allowed us to be in your protagonist's life for around forty pages (forty *contiguous* pages), we will have forged a strong connection with her, and you can safely hop us over to a brand-new character, story line, and situation. We'll hold on to our bond with your primary hero. Now, you'll need to come back to our hero after not more than, say, twenty-five pages in another story line, and you'll need to keep coming back to our main character consistently after cutting away. But so long as you allow us to maintain our relationship with your protagonist, we'll be fine with you taking us on side trips with other characters.

Sometimes people hear me teach this, and they misunderstand. I'm not saying your hero is the only character who can be onstage during these forty pages. And I'm not saying you can't intercut between story lines in your novel. Nor am I saying that you can't yet introduce other people who will end up being viewpoint characters for your story. You can have seven viewpoint characters for your novel, and you can have all seven onstage at one time right from the beginning. But we can see through only the main character's eyes for those first forty contiguous pages.

Like I said, a prologue is a freebie. An exception. If you want to take several pages to prepare the ground for the main story, even if that means we don't meet the hero yet, go for it. Readers understand that a prologue is in a different category from the rest. We sort of withhold our love from those characters (if it's a villain, anyway). When it's over and we meet the hero, then we start making our connections.

However, if your prologue shows a sympathetic character, we'll begin bonding with that person. And the more pages you give us in that person's story, the stronger the bond will become. Use that dynamic to your advantage, like by making us care about someone who later becomes a villain you want us to still hold out hope for. Just realize that it's happening. The longer we stay in one story line, the more we will assume this is the main one.

A special case is a novel with dual protagonists. This forty contiguous pages rule (er, guideline) applies even to a story with more than one protagonist.

In a case like that, you must choose. One protagonist must be featured first. Like it or not, that character will be seen as the main hero, even if in your mind they are equals. You can almost completely balance the scales throughout the rest of the novel by giving the second hero more and more scenes, but always in the back of the reader's mind, that first hero will be the alpha. That's okay. Use it to your advantage. As they say in computer programming, it's not a bug; it's a feature.

By Darkness Hid by Jill Williamson has dual protagonists. Originally, the author had intercut their scenes quite a bit during the first fifty pages. It was all good writing, but in her effort to split the reader's affection between the two heroes, she ended up making the reader's affection simply split. As in *leave.* Our solution was to pack several of one hero's scenes together in a line in part one. Then in part two we went back in time to virtually the same moment, but this time we saw what happened in the other hero's scenes.

Finally, Hero B's scenes caught up to where we'd left off with Hero A. From that point on, we intercut between the two heroes however the author wished. But because we'd had around forty pages in Hero A's life before cutting to Hero B, our bond with the first one remained. And then, because we were given around forty contiguous pages in Hero B's life, we built a strong connection with that hero, too. By the time Jill began intercutting between the two, we loved them both equally.

But notice that it was the refusal to intercut too early that allowed this to happen. You must stay with your protagonist for the first forty contiguous pages of your book (excepting a prologue) in order for your reader to build a connection strong enough to bear it when you do finally cut away to someone new.

Now, don't be legalistic about this. There's nothing magical about having exactly forty pages. You can go probably as few as twenty-five in one story line and be okay. And you probably wouldn't want to go more than seventy-five pages before cutting away if you *are* going to cut away. Waiting until page 200 to cut to a new story line will be disruptive for the reader, who has come to understand that there will be no other story lines.

This goes back to my mixed metaphor of plant and payoff. Whatever you're going to be doing later in the book, you need to set up toward the beginning. That doesn't mean you have to introduce every viewpoint character in the first seventy-five pages. But it does mean that you need to cut away at least once or twice in those pages to show the reader *that you're going to have* other viewpoint characters and story lines.

I'm hoping this forty-pages guideline won't seem onerous to you. I've given you so much to do with the main character in the first fifty pages that you almost can't do it all if you jump over to one or more other viewpoint characters during that time. But I want to stress one more time that it only helps you to let your reader stay in the headspace of your protagonist for forty pages in a row. If connecting the reader with the hero is Job One in the first fifty pages, and if staying with the hero is the way to allow that connection to grow, it's as close to giving a rule as I'll come in this book.

❧• INTRODUCING DUAL PROTAGONISTS •❧

Since we're already on the subject, let's finish talking about how to introduce your co-heroes.

Down With Love features dual protagonists: Barbara Novak and Catcher Block (played by Renée Zellweger and Ewan McGregor, respectively). First we meet Barbara, who has come to New York City to meet her editor and the publisher of her radical new best-selling book, *Down With Love*. We see the darling little country girl pushed about by the bustling masses of Manhattan. We see her stand before the executives from the publishing house—all men, of course—and explain to them the thesis of her book, which makes them more than a little nervous. But Barbara stands her ground, and we love her immediately.

Then we meet Catcher Block, "Ladies' Man, Man's Man, Man About Town," flying in on a helicopter with three dancing girls from the Copa floor show. He's Mr. Stud if ever there was one. We hear him regale his own editor with tales of his exploits, and we see how the women throw themselves at Catcher. Try as we might, we can't help liking him, either.

By the end of Catcher's introduction, we have two heroes we're very connected to, and we can't wait to see how these two irresistible forces are going to collide.

There's really no trick to introducing co-heroes in a novel. Just craft a special introductory scene for each of your heroes. Don't introduce Hero 2 until you've given us forty pages in the life of Hero 1, but then just bring on the second hero. In the same way that you'll create a scene to bring on the villain and your other major characters, create one to perfectly introduce your second protagonist.

❧ THEME ❧

If you have a theme or message in your novel, we need to begin seeing it in the first fifty pages.

Brainstorm a dozen ways to show off primary, secondary, and opposite facets of your theme, and see how many of them you can elegantly work into those opening spreads. You don't have to cram them all in—you've got over three hundred pages to explore your theme, after all—but just be sure you've begun planting those seeds early on.

Such things make rereading a novel especially fun, because the second time through, knowing where the book is going, you see things the author was doing to set us up for it, though we couldn't see them the first time. I like watching *Back to the Future* for this reason. In the early section of the film—equivalent to most of the first fifty pages in a novel, I'd say—the filmmakers were planting so many things that would come to have importance later. It's a testimony to their prowess as storytellers that they were giving us the theme from the outset.

Another great example of this is *Invictus*. The very first scene of the movie shows two ball fields divided by a road. On one side, the rich whites play rugby on a nice field with well-kempt buildings around. On the other side, poor blacks play soccer on a patch of dead grass surrounded by tenements. And right down the middle road comes Nelson Mandela. It was a powerful statement of the movie's primary theme.

If your novel has a theme, how can you illustrate it in these first fifty pages?

❧· CIRCULARITY ·❧

Circularity concerns how something at the end can refer back to the beginning, and vice versa.

The writers for the TV show *Grey's Anatomy* like to use circularity. Episodes often begin with a character narrating on a particular subject, like choices. And then at the end, the same character reprises the subject of choices to close the show.

Circularity is a brilliant device for making a story feel like a unified whole. It also makes it seem that the story was perfectly formed and intentional before the first moment had transpired in it. It feels to the reader that you, the author, knew what you were doing all along. Which is great, because the process of writing a novel usually has more in common with stumbling along trying to find your way than it does with anything preformed in perfection.

You can practice circularity in ways large and small. At the end of your novel, if you refer back to how the novel began, you'll be employing circularity on a large scale. But you can also use it on a smaller scale, perhaps as bookends to a scene.

The opening scene of one of my novels (*Operation: Firebrand*) begins and ends with the same line. The first line of the book has one meaning when the reader encounters it. But by the end of the scene, virtually the same words have a vastly different connotation. That's circularity on a small scale.

In your first fifty pages, you can't really do anything about circularity on a large scale. That will have to wait until the end, when you come back and refer to something from these opening pages. But you can certainly file it in your mind that this thing you're writing to in the first fifty pages is something you definitely want to hearken back to later.

Circularity makes your story seem skillfully wrought. Try it in your novel.

❧· PLANTING FOR A HARVEST ·❧

As we have seen, in your first fifty pages you will be laying the groundwork for what is to come. Indeed, one of the main purposes of these pages is to allow the main story to begin.

Throughout these early pages you will be setting things up for later. You will be establishing situations, relationships, and history, all of which will be called upon in the rest of the story. Plant, plant, plant. Off you go, Johnny Appleseed.

If your hero will need to be an expert skier at some important point in the novel, you'd better set that up in the first fifty pages. (Not through *telling,* of course, but through action, scene, dialogue, dumb puppets, and/or arguments. Right?) If your hero is an expert on ancient Akkadian cuneiform, we'd better learn that in the first fifty pages.

This is plant and payoff. Anything major that you'll need to harvest later, you need to plant now at the outset. Not on page 1, necessarily, but certainly by page 50.

This is referring to large items pertaining to plot and character. I don't mean that if in your climactic scene you have a hairbrush on a dresser you have to find a place in the first fifty pages to establish that hairbrush. But we just can't be finding out on page 400 that the hero speaks fluent Farsi just in time to read the key bit of paperwork and thus save the day. Um, no.

So plant, my dear gardener. And if you're *on* page 400 and you realize the hero needs to speak Farsi, go back to pages 1 through

50 and find a place to naturally reveal this, okay? Plant now for a harvest later.

❧• WELL AND TRULY BEGIN •❧

I mentioned this earlier, but it bears repeating: begin your novel with a good long scene. Eight to twenty pages, I'd say. None of these one- or two-page "scenes," not to begin your book.

It's the same dynamic at play as in the first forty contiguous pages of your novel. You want your book to look like it begins right where you meant it to begin, right where there was something meaty and significant to reveal. Do it like a short film or short story. Make it stand alone, with all the dynamics of beginning, middle, and end.

Don't tiptoe into your book. Launch the thing with a major dance number.

Well and truly begin.

❧• THE FIRST FIFTY PAGES OF A SEQUEL •❧

Nearly everything I've talked about in this book has been with the assumption that you're writing a standalone novel or book one of a series. Such is not always the case, of course. So what adjustments do you need to make if this is not book one?

Actually, not many. To build a solid structure for a novel's beginning, you do the same things for book thirty-one as you do for book one. The tasks are the same: introduce the hero, establish normal, show the hero's initial state, etc.

However, in latter books in a series you can use some shorthand. If book two features the same hero as in book one, you don't need to take as long to introduce her as you did the first time. If the villain is the same, book two might just need an update on what he's up to, and not a full introductory special. If book two shows the hero still on his inner journey, you don't need to go back and show his initial state again. However, a scene showing his condition at this particular point on the way might be in order.

A special case is when your books are really one long story that has been cut up into two or more portions just to keep the thing from being a brick. Like *The Lord of the Rings*. But even there, I'd recommend you take a look at the end of book one and the beginning of each subsequent book and craft a little "getting reacquainted" scene to reorient your reader. You don't know how long it's been since she read the previous book in the series, after all.

Besides, beginnings are fun to write, even if they're smaller, as in a case like this.

So just take a look at what you've got going. Pretend you're telling this story to a class of college students, and you had to stop midway through for spring break. When you come back, they pretty much remember what was happening last time, but a little "as you recall" refresher scene would be fun.

My *Operation: Firebrand* series spans three novels. Each stands alone, but the same group of main characters is featured in all three. In books two and three, I created full introductory chapters to get the reader reacquainted with their personalities and relationships. It wasn't as if I thought the reader wouldn't remember. It was as if I knew I might have new readers for this book who hadn't read book one. And even for those readers who had been with me every time, they needed a scene to catch them up with what the heroes were up to as *this* story begins.

If you're writing book two or beyond in a series, go back through *The First 50 Pages* and view every chapter through that lens. You won't need to give it the full treatment like you did with book one, but you should still address just about every teaching point in this book. What I've presented here is what makes for a solid beginning for a novel. And that's something you want for book one, two, two hundred, and every book in between.

And now, how to begin is near its end.

CHAPTER 14
CONCLUSION

Now this is not the end. It is not even the beginning of the end. But it is, perhaps, the end of the beginning. —WINSTON CHURCHILL

WHO KNEW SO MUCH COULD BE SAID ABOUT SO few pages?

When we started out, you probably had some excellent ideas for how a novel's opening spreads ought to go. You've no doubt encountered some terrific beginnings, both in fiction and in cinema, and it's likely you had an inkling of how you'd like to begin your book. Maybe you'd written out a draft of it—or even the full manuscript.

What I hope I've brought to you is a schematic by which you can evaluate a novel's first fifty pages—yours or other people's. I've worked to give you the tools that will help you not only know what ought to go into those pages but also how to build them with your own hands.

We began our time together by spelunking into the mysterious reaches of the mind of an acquisitions editor and agent. We saw the conditions and expectations under which they operate, which hopefully helped you perceive publishers with a greater understanding. We saw 101 things *not* to do in your first pages if you want to keep the positive attention of these editors and agents.

Then we spent the bulk of the book looking at what *to* do to craft a tremendous opening for your novel that will serve as both the structural cornerstone for a book built right and the device that will enable your reader to receive the whole novel in precisely the way you intended.

Very little of what I've said should be considered as the only right way to do something. I've got some pretty strong ideas for what works best (No, Jeff … really?), but that doesn't mean other ideas aren't just as valid. And, obviously, plenty of novelists who don't do a lick of what I say are enjoying blockbuster sales. [*shrugs*] *C'est la vie.*

All I ask is that you carefully consider what I've said at each juncture. What I've laid out here has resulted in novels that have won or been finalists for most of the major awards in my corner of publishing. Again, that doesn't mean my way is the only way.

But it does mean it works.

My goal is to empower you, not constrain you. I want you to feel equipped to write any of thousands of ways to begin a novel. Knowing the components involved and the tasks set before a novel's first fifty pages will arm you to accomplish those things any way you please.

So go out and write incredible novels … with outstanding fifty-page starts.

❧· TAKE US HOME, JACK ·❧

The Texas sun continued to burn down on President John F. Kennedy and his listeners on that day in 1962. With the crowd in the palm of his hand, Jack cast the vision—and threw down the gauntlet—for the space program.

"If I were to say, my fellow citizens, that we shall send to the moon—240,000 miles away, from the control station in Houston—a giant rocket more than three hundred feet tall ... made of new metal alloys, some of which have not yet been invented ... fitted together with a precision better than the finest watch, carrying all the equipment needed for ... survival, on an untried mission to an unknown celestial body, and then return it safely to Earth ... and do all this and do it right, and do it first, before this decade is out, *then we must be bold.*"

You, too, dear writer, must be bold. Hear these heroes of beginnings calling you to glory:

- Alberto Salazar said, "Standing on the starting line, we're all cowards."
- "So many fail because they don't get started—they don't go," W. Clement Stone said. "They don't overcome inertia. They don't begin."
- "You will never win if you never begin," said Helen Rowland.
- Martin Luther King, Jr.: "Take the first step in faith. You don't have to see the whole staircase, just take the first step."
- Alan Cohen: "Do not wait until the conditions are perfect to begin. Beginning makes the conditions perfect."
- And Johann Wolfgang von Goethe: "Whatever you do or dream you can do—begin it. Boldness has genius and power and magic in it."

So crank up "Jack Sparrow" from the soundtrack of *Pirates of the Caribbean: Dead Man's Chest* (or whatever gets you in the mood to write your novel), call up the notes you've taken and the brainstorms you've had during our time together, and start.

"All this will not be finished in the first one hundred days," President Kennedy said that day in Texas. "Nor will it be finished in the first thousand days, nor in the life of this administration, nor even perhaps in our lifetime on this planet. But let us begin."

INDEX

Printed in the United States
by Baker & Taylor Publisher Services